Micro-teach Masterclass

(black & white edition)

Preparing and delivering your micro-teach for the Award in Education and Training and for interviews in teaching

Nabeel Zaidi, LLB (Hons), LLM, Pg. Dip., DMS, MBA, Cert. Ed., Barrister

About this book

Micro-teaching is an essential component of the Award in Education and Training and is often used during the interview and selection process at learning providers for lecturing and training positions. This textbook provides detailed practical guidance and a step-by-step approach to researching, planning, delivering and evaluating a micro-teach intended for the Award in Education and Training course and for interviews at learning providers. A worked example is used to demonstrate the process in action. Several references are made to online resources that can be accessed free of charge and which demonstrate particular features of an effective micro-teach within a professional context and delivered by experts in their field. This textbook is unique in its detailed practical treatment and approach of the subject. It should assist in preparing candidates for an effective micro-teach in their course and during job interviews for teaching and training positions. This textbook complements the following textbooks by the same author: *Achieving your Award in Education and Training: The Comprehensive Course Companion* and *Achieving your Award in Education and Training: The Comprehensive Course Companion (Special Edition)*.

About the author

Nabeel has been in the further education sector since 1996, occupying various lecturing, middle and senior management and consultancy roles, including working with several awarding organisations, undertaking quality assurance assignments, delivering professional training to the education sector on equality and diversity and the Ofsted common inspection framework and developing and delivering on undergraduate and post-graduate business management programmes and teaching qualifications. He is also a Reviewer for the Quality Assurance Agency (QAA) and runs his own college and consultancy company. He has published a number of textbooks relating to teaching.

Nabeel holds various academic and professional qualifications and titles, including being a qualified Barrister, an MBA in Educational Management (University of Leicester), a Certificate in Education (Institute of Education), a Post-Graduate Diploma in Professional Legal Skills (Inns of Court School of Law / City University), a Master's degree in Law (University College London), a degree in Law (Queen Mary's College, University of London), and a Post-Graduate Diploma in Management Studies.

Contents

Origins of micro-teaching

Origins: micro-teaching originated from Stanford University, USA in 1963, where it was introduced to provide a more effective means of initial teacher training.

Definition: micro-teaching can be defined as a teaching situation lasting between 4-20 minutes, delivered to between 3-10 learners, following which pre-service teachers receive immediate feedback on the effectiveness of their session. **Rationale:** the rationale for micro-teaching was as follows:

- to provide a real teaching experience;
- to reduce the complexities of a full teaching session, thereby providing pre-service teachers with more control of their environment;
- to use immediate performance-related feedback to inform professional development;
- to allow pre-service teachers to select a topic for delivery that they were most competent in; and
- to increase skills development through practice and feedback.

Uses: pre-service teachers were provided with some training before they undertook a micro-teach session, which was often delivered to their peers, and based on their preferred topic or subject area. This was videotaped or audio recorded and their supervisor provided them with feedback on their performance, assisting them to analyse the strengths and weaknesses of the session and discuss how the session might be improved. In many instances, peers also provided feedback on the session.[1]

---

[1] Cooper & Allen (02/1970): *Microteaching: History and Present Status*, DHEW

▶▶ Fast forward to 2015

Developments: micro-teaching continues to play an important part in pre-service teacher training. It forms a pivotal component of the Award in Education and Training unit entitled: *Understanding and Using Inclusive Teaching and Learning Approaches in Education and Training*. While the overall model of micro-teaching from 1963 remains in tact, there have been a number of changes in the UK in approaches to teaching, learning and assessment. For instance, in the last 15 years there has been a noticeable shift towards a greater focus on learning that takes place in a session.

Therefore, a good session should have evidence of new learning taking place, be more learner-centred with less didactic, teacher-centred delivery. There should also be regular checking of learning. These changes have implications for your assessed micro-teach (i.e. your planning, delivery and assessment strategies). It has even more profound implications for when you prepare and deliver a micro-teach as part of a teacher / trainer-related job interview.

Both the Award in Education and Training and the further education and skills sector expect teachers to be self-evaluative and self-reflective of their practice, being able to identify strengths and areas for development. Knowledge about awarding organisation, inspection and review body requirements and expectations can also prove to be influential during a job interview, since your teaching, learning and assessment practices will need to be aligned to such expectations as they affect inspection and awarding organisation reporting.

Preparatory considerations

Selecting a topic: although there are a wide range of topics that are appropriate and can be selected for a micro-teach, you need to consider a number of factors before deciding on a final topic to deliver, most of which are considered below.

Resourcing

- Are there sufficient physical resources? For instance, you might be considering delivering a cooking demonstration, but is a kitchen available for this purpose? and what about health and safety considerations?

- Are there sufficient technical resources and are they compatible? For example, do you need a data projector, internet access and speakers?

- Are the resources safe? If your micro-teach includes the use of bio-chemicals, will it comply with the learning provider's health and safety policy and procedure?

- If your micro-teach is going to be outdoors or off-site, what contingency measures do you need to take in case things do not go according to plan (e.g. change in weather during an outdoor micro-teach)?

- Have you estimated printing and related costs?

- Have you factored-in for extra handouts? For instance, some of your audience might need new assessment handouts due to misunderstanding the instructions and completing the handouts incorrectly.

- If the micro-teach is part of a job interview, have you checked that the organisation is able to provide you with the resources that you need and whether these are technically compatible (e.g. you might be using different software or different versions that are not fully compatible)?

- What if the electronic resources fail on the day or there are technical issues, do you have an alternative (e.g. handouts of your PowerPoint slides in case the data projector fails)?

- Do the resources take account of the individual needs of the audience (e.g. are they adapted for learners with disclosed disabilities and learning difficulties)?

- Have you involved your audience (peers / learners) in the assessment process (i.e. asked them what learning materials or resources they would prefer to use)? For instance, if you are demonstrating a particular product, do they want to handle or use that product as well while you are demonstrating it? and if so, do you have more than one example of that product, and is such handling or use likely to increase engagement and learning?

- Are these resources going to be included in your lesson plan?

Audience knowledge

- How much of your topic do learners already know? Remember, you should be demonstrating new learning during a micro-teach (this is less relevant for a job interview, since an interview pack will normally provide you with an outline of how to treat the learners). If you are delivering a topic that all your audience already know, it will be very difficult to demonstrate new learning taking place and your audience may engage less as a result.

- Your audience might have different levels of knowledge or experience of your topic area. It would be useful to ask audience members with knowledge and experience of your topic to share some of it during the session. This ought to increase learner engagement, participation and be more learner-centred.

- Are there any members of the audience that know more about your topic than you do and can you consult them about your topic? Are they willing to give you some guidance (e.g. how your topic works in industry, such as current practice)?

- Even if your audience has no knowledge or experience of your topic area, they are likely to be working at a different pace during your micro-teach (i.e. some members might understand concepts or information faster than others). How will you adjust your differentiation strategies accordingly during the planning and delivery stages of your micro-teach?

Audience interest

- Have you consulted your proposed audience for the micro-teach in order to identify their level of interest in the topic you intend to deliver? Audience engagement and active participation are important. Delivering a topic that is of interest to your proposed audience is likely to increase engagement, participation and learning.

- Are there any particular topics that your proposed audience would like to see delivered? If you are having difficulty in selecting a topic for your micro-teach, they may have some useful suggestions that you could consider.

Topic length or complexity

- Do you intend to deliver an entire topic or a small, yet important part of a topic? For instance, delivering a session on how to use a digital camera might be too broad, while demonstrating a particular technique using a specific lens should be sufficiently narrow, yet suitable for a micro-teach. Another example is make-up; this topic area is so broad that it could be covered in a dedicated course, while outlining one small aspect of make-up, such as drawing eyebrows, might be appropriate.

- How complex is your topic area and do you have the expertise to deliver the topic in a short time span? What amounts to a complex topic is a relative question. It really depends on your

audience's existing knowledge and experience. For instance, delivering a session outlining the treatments for dementia might be too complex for an audience without any knowledge or experience of it and without a medical background to follow it, yet it might be wholly appropriate to an audience which possesses a medical background and/or have cared for a relative with dementia.

Own level of knowledge

- How confident are you in your existing knowledge of your proposed topic?

- Is your knowledge and experience current? If not, how can you ensure currency?

- Even if you possess a degree of expertise in your topic, how will you deliver it to ensure that all your audience understands the topic you are delivering? For instance, you might know most of the current Search Engine Optimisation (SEO) techniques. Even if you focus on one small and simple area of SEO, how will you present the information in an engaging way so that your audience members, who have not previously designed a detailed website, can follow your examination of SEO?

Topics peers are delivering

- Do you know what topics your peers will be delivering for their micro-teach? If you do, you can do one of two things: (i) select a different topic, or (ii) choose a different aspect of the same topic (e.g. if a colleague is delivering a session on how to make apple crumble, you might decide to outline how to make rhubarb crumble and use it as an opportunity to compare notes on how each of you will be approaching the delivery of your topic).

- In some cases, such as job interviews for teaching positions, you may be given a brief, with a specific topic to deliver as part of the micro-teach. In such a situation, preparation is key and delivering the topic in a highly engaging and, to some extent, innovative manner is likely to be more important than the topic itself. Imagine if the panel are interviewing eight candidates on the same day; they will be viewing eight micro-teach sessions. How will you ensure that yours impresses them on the day?

Preparatory steps

It can be difficult sometimes to decide on a topic to deliver for the micro-teach. You may have narrowed the selection to three or more topics and you may even have gone through the initial thoughts above, but it is not until you start actively working through preparatory steps that you will realise the most appropriate micro-teach topic to deliver. So, what are those preparatory steps? Outlined below are some of the steps you can undertake, based on what we have considered so far.

Step 1

Identify five possible topic areas that you could deliver as a micro-teach.

Step 2

Check whether you have sufficient knowledge, information and experience to deliver those topic areas.

Step 3

Select up to three topics out of the five that you are confident in researching and delivering.

Step 4

Consult with your peers or prospective audience about which topics they like out of your short-list of topics.

Step 5

Discuss with your peers what topics they are delivering so that yours does not significantly overlap with theirs. Naturally, you could deliver on the exact same topic area as a colleague, but if you are delivering after them, are the audience likely to be as engaging or interested in the topic? Will they be learning something new?

Step 6

Discuss your short-list of topics with your tutor and take on board any advice or suggestions they provide.

Step 7

Start researching your three topic areas and critically evaluate them. Then select one of the topics for the micro-teach. This might seem a cumbersome process, but imagine if you selected one topic from the start and, based on research, realised that there was insufficient information available to deliver an effective session or you discovered you were not confident in delivering it. If you have a choice of at least three topics, then this should minimise the risk of going through the process again.

Step 8

Identify your audience's level of existing knowledge, interest and any individual learning needs for your selected topic.

Step 9

Produce an outline of what you will deliver in the session. This can be in the form of flow diagrams, mind maps, notes or any other form that makes sense to you. Also consider how long each segment of the topic is likely to take, the resources you are likely to need and the teaching, learning and assessment strategies you might employ at each stage of the process. This is a preparatory step before you start drafting your lesson plan. This process should make it easier to draft a more effective lesson plan. We will look at step 8 in more detail in the next few pages, with a worked example. (Incidentally, step 9 should also prove very useful to anyone preparing a micro-teach for a job interview, since you need to be clear about your rationale and you might be asked questions about various aspects of your micro-teach.)

Worked micro-teach example

Selecting an effective title for your micro-teach

CREATING A BOKEH EFFECT ('BACKGROUND BLURRING') USING A DSLR CAMERA AND A 50 MM F1.8 PORTRAIT LENS

This can be selected as the title for an audience that is familiar with DSLR cameras and understands the basics of different types of lenses, hence the technical nature of the title. If the audience has not used a DSLR camera before, the title could be made less technical, such as:

LEARN TO PHOTOGRAPH LIKE A PROFESSIONAL, WITH BACKGROUND BLURRING

Both titles refer to the same topic area to be covered, namely bokeh / background blurring, but the approach is made less technical in the second title. What can we learn from expert presenters? Well, it's about using content and techniques that attract and engage the audience ... a lot has to do with the 'pitch'. A persuasive presentation is likely to generate interest, enquiries and sales for a company. Similarly, getting the pitch right for your audience is likely to improve their attention, increase their engagement and participation and most likely improve their learning. Naturally, you would not stop at the title; there would be adjustments all the way through to take account of your learners' existing knowledge and individual needs.

So what about job interviews for teaching positions? How important do you think the title, content and style of your micro-teach presentation and learning materials are for the interview?

Imagine for a moment that you are on the panel of interviewers and you have already watched five micro-teach presentations on the exact same topic (learning providers usually specify a particular subject topic so that they can compare candidate responses, so as to ensure that the selection process is fair). A distinctive and innovative approach to the presentation and delivery of the topic is likely to generate more interest among the interviewers than one that just delivers the subject content. After all, learners (especially those under 30 years old) have become more demanding, being accustomed to high quality media content and access to instant information delivered across many platforms.

I recall in 2009 a colleague approached me who worked at the same further education college as myself. She asked me to advise her on the best approach to preparing a presentation for her interview for a course coordinator role at the college. I recommended that she focus her presentation on identifying and demonstrating the impact of teaching, learning and assessment strategies on learners for her programme.

The concept of 'impact' was relatively new at the time among senior managers, mainly because of its introduction in the 2009 Ofsted Common Inspection Framework. She delivered the presentation, following which there was complete silence from the interview panel for approximately thirty seconds and the panel only asked one or two questions.

She was appointed to the role of course coordinator the same day. It later transpired that the interview panel had devised the questions around the concept of 'impact', which she had already delivered in detail during her presentation. She had in effect, with assistance from myself, anticipated the needs, interests and expectations of the interview panel.

Therefore, there are a number of similarities between a presentation and a micro-teach, and many of the skills are transferable, especially if you intend to become a trainer, delivering workshops and other events to delegates. From my personal experience of delivering professional training and workshops around the UK, I focused more extensively on learning than I did during teaching sessions. This is because I had delegates that wanted to learn complex facts in a short time frame and be able to take the information back and train their staff and teams. I also used session objectives and learning checks throughout the one day workshops. Feedback used to take the form of written evaluations.

Sometimes it is better to revisit the title of the micro-teach together with the introduction once the session has been planned and resources identified and allocated. The title can then better reflect the content to be delivered. After all, the initial focus of your topic might change, based on your interests and research, making any initial title less accurate (unless of course, you possess expertise in that area to begin with, in which case your title and introduction are likely to be precise from the outset).

Resource requirements

- a cropped frame DSLR camera,

- a 50 mm, f 1.8 prime lens,

- 2 laptops with 2 SD card readers, 4 SD cards, HDMI cable and PowerPoint (one laptop for own use during delivery and shared with learners during the learning activity), connection to the data projector,

- Internet access to play back relevant video clips from You Tube,

- an additional DSLR camera, with a 50 mm, f 1.8 prime lens and laptop with SD card reader, if available for the audience to use,

- a data projector and screen to display the PowerPoint presentation and photographs taken during the session,

- sufficient copies of handouts and written assessments,

- a selection of everyday and interesting objects to take photographs of indoors and/or outdoors,

- tables on which to place the objects to be photographed, with different depths of field (i.e. with varying distances for their backgrounds - this directly affects the extend of the background blurring),

- handouts of the PowerPoint slides, with space next to each slide for the audience to take notes,

- a sample of professionally taken photographs from newspapers and magazines demonstrating background blurring (most often found in sports photography, such as pictures of footballers on the football pitch),

- You Tube video clips demonstrating 'bokeh' techniques.[1]

[1] E.g. https://www.youtube.com/watch?v=qPcdWxhLwoA
https://www.youtube.com/watch?v=mP1ubIs2vQg

Rationale for selecting these resources

- It is a practical subject, hence learning can be maximised using photographic equipment. The selected lens produces a good level of background blurring and is not expensive to purchase, while the DSLR camera should have the capability of taking full advantage of the lens's features. Flash photography is not being used, since the lens is capable of low light photography. Flash photography might be relevant to techniques demonstrating wedding photography or maximising the softness of the background blurring, which is for more advanced users (it will also be difficult or time consuming to set-up);

- An additional camera, lens and laptop should make learning faster, since the presenter can demonstrate how to use the camera, while the audience can mimic the instructions using a similar camera. The laptop with SD card reader is to be used to display the photographs taken, while the spare laptop with SD card reader is for the audience to view their results. This should also encourage group working and independent learning;

- The tables, positioned at different distances from a background (e.g. wall and/or other objects), will have a direct effect on the depth of field and amount of background blurring achieved;

- The need for everyday and interesting objects to photograph is important, because background blurring with this type of prime lens can make even a bottle of water look interesting. This should surprise the audience members unfamiliar with this technique and engage and motivate them further;

- A selection of professional photographs, taken from newspapers and magazines, demonstrate this technique's relevance to everyday media we view;

- Internet access to relevant you tube videos of how bokeh is used by amateur and professional photographers should make the delivery more engaging, while also appealing to audience members with a preference for visual and kinaesthetic learning styles;

- Outdoor photographs should make the session more dynamic and provide opportunities for the audience to experiment with the new technique they have just learnt. Again, this is likely to appeal most to audience members with a preference for visual and kinaesthetic learning styles.

Differentiated resources

- Resources will need to be differentiated if some audience members already use a DSLR camera and portrait lens or undertake basic photography and have the potential to complete tasks early;

- Extension activities can be designed to take account of audience members who learn the tasks very quickly. For instance, the next logical photographic technique after bokeh is selective focusing, which also uses bokeh, but allows the user to decide which object or area to have in focus, thereby resulting in the blurring of other objects, depending on how close they are to the lens;

- Where such extension activities are being planned, the audience members affected could work on their own while others are continuing to learn the technique and use an extension handout which outlines the steps to taking photographs with selective focusing.

Examples of photographs and videos to be used for demonstrating bokeh and selective focusing

In photograph 1, the female subject is in focus, while the background is blurred. This is one example of bokeh.

Photograph 2 is of a bottle of water, shot using a Canon DSLR 600D camera, with a Canon 50 mm f 1.8 prime lens, set at f 1.8. As you can see, the bottle is clearly in focus, while the background is completely blurred.

Photograph 3 is an example of selective focusing. The female at the front is sharply in focus, while her colleagues in the background are slightly out of focus.

needs to be shown. Audience members can then watch the remainder in their own time.

https://www.youtube.com/watch?v=mP1ubIs2vQg

You Tube video 2 shows a range of lenses and how lighting affects bokeh. It is a professional photoshoot in New York's Times Square. It is more technical than the first You Tube video, but a lot more exciting and provides a glimpse into how professionals make use of photographic equipment and lighting to shoot effective bokeh images.

Photograph 4 is an example of selective focusing, with a slowed down shutter speed. The camera was mounted on a tripod. The man standing absolutely still just outside the tube station is clearly in focus, while those moving in the shot have been blurred due to the slow shutter speed. This can be considered as a further extension activity.

The following are screenshots of You Tube resources that could be selectively incorporated (i.e. short extracts) into this micro-teach.

https://www.youtube.com/watch?v=qPcdWxhLwoA

Video 1 is a good You Tube video for demonstrating bokeh and lighting conditions. It uses everyday household objects to create stunning bokeh effects. It should be a good resource since it demonstrates effective use of the technique. Only a small extract

https://www.youtube.com/watch?v=Ldcs4zn92ra

You Tube video 3 is very informative and presented by a photographer and reviewer of photographic equipment. The content will appeal to a range of audiences, but there are expletives and some spoken sexual references made in the video, so content needs to be sensitively extracted/used in order to avoid such content being played. The photo shoots take place in Hong Kong, so it makes the topic even more interesting.

https://www.youtube.com/watch?v=smox9eGs-GI

You Tube video 4 examines selective focus. It is likely to be useful as an extension activity for audience members who have completed the bokeh related tasks early or who are more advanced in their photography.

https://www.youtube.com/watch?v=kGud8vGwp-Y

You Tube Video 5 introduces the topic of shutter speed and would be a good extension activity for more advanced users.

Further photographic and video resources can be found through an online search for free images, by looking at stock image websites, some of which permit free downloads (albeit with water marked photographs), by taking your own photographs using different levels of bokeh. At this point in the resources search, you should be compiling a range of references or links for further information that the audience can refer to after the micro-teach, should they so desire.

Initial review of resources

As you can see, we now have a number of photographic and video resources focusing on bokeh and extension activities that include selective focusing and adjustments to shutter speed. Assuming that we have access to the photographic equipment, a laptop, data projector, tables and objects, do you think we have sufficient information and resources to make this a viable topic to deliver as a micro-teach?

Assuming that the audience members are mixed ability users of digital cameras, then there are sufficient resources to meet individual learner resource needs. We have also considered some resource related differentiation strategies, which can be included in the lesson plan later on.

More importantly, the range of photographic and video resources available should make it an engaging session. The location settings in the videos are varied, as are presentation styles, content and approach. There should be something here of interest for all the audience members. If there are one or two advanced users of digital photography in the audience, they could be asked to bring in samples of their photography and briefly share their practical experience during the session (as and when prompted).

When you are called for a job interview for a teaching or training position you may only have a few days to prepare for the interview, with the micro-teach being one element of the interview. Therefore, the method that has been outlined should provide you with a structure and systematic approach that makes effective and efficient use of valuable preparation time.

You could also be making notes at this stage regarding the order in which the resources will be used, who they are targeting in the audience, how much of the micro-teach session they will occupy and possible checks on learning linked to the resources. (This last point will become clearer during the preparation section of this textbook).

Once you have collected the key resources for your micro-teach session, you should be outlining the outcomes you expect learners to achieve during your session. At this point, we will not look at command verbs nor will we arrive at a clear set of outcomes, since these may well change by the time you draft your lesson plan. You may end up discarding or substituting some of the outcomes due to timing or other constraints or as a result of further consulting the audience members of your micro-teach or your tutor.

The expected outcomes for this micro-teach session can be divided into 'beginner level' and 'advanced level'. In other words, what you expect the audience members to be able to achieve during the session, according to existing knowledge, experience and ability. This is assuming that they have accurately communicated these to you during initial consultation and discussion about your micro-teach topic. Be prepared for variations either way (i.e. under-estimating their existing knowledge, experience and ability and over-estimating it). The principal advantage of categorising the outcomes in this way is to ensure that you are differentiating and planning to meet individual learner needs.

Beginner level expected outcomes from learners

During the session, **all** beginner level learners will:

- be able to use auto focus on an object near to them, ensuring that there is sufficient distance from any other background objects, such as walls and furniture;

- be able to take a basic photograph with background blurring evident;

- be able to outline basic principles of creating bokeh / background blurring effects.

The quality of photographs produced by beginner level learners are likely:

- to have some imperfections, such as minor blurring of the object that is supposed to be in focus, perhaps due to camera shake that the camera could not technically compensate for;

- to be over or under-exposed due to lighting considerations not being taken into account when composing and taking the photograph.

The level of understanding demonstrated is likely to be as follows:

- the outline of the principles of creating bokeh may be fragmented. For instance, the notion of depth of field might not be fully understood, but statements might be made to the effect that there should be some distance from the object and background for bokeh, but little consideration given to the proximity of the object to the lens, given that it is not a zoom lens;

- technical language might not be used or used correctly, but the overall principles are understood.

Advanced level expected outcomes from learners

During the session, **all** advanced level learners will:

- be able to make effective use of depth of field when comprising and taking a shot with background blurring;

- demonstrate an awareness of effective lighting conditions for bokeh;

- be able to use selective focusing.

During the session, **some** advanced level learners will:

- be able to use different shutter speeds with or without bokeh elements;

- be able to adjust shutter speeds when photographing a moving object or compensating for low lighting conditions;

- be able to use manual features of the camera and lens when taking shots with bokeh elements and selective focusing.

The quality of photographs produced by advanced level learners are likely:

- to have good quality bokeh, including:

  - the object that is supposed to be in focus, being in sharp focus, with minor blurring at different depths where the object has significant three dimensional depth;

  - any spot lighting elements in the background to have a pleasant round or soft bokeh effect (see example below);

  - use of different f-stops, such as f 2.8 to maximise sharpness of the object in focus and a softer blurring of the background;

- to have effective selective focusing, with the proposed object to be in focus being sharply in focus. The learner might even have used different f-stops to vary the sharpness and background blurring;

- to have photographs with different shutter speeds that:

  - compensate or take advantage of different lighting conditions (e.g. slower shutter speed for low lighting conditions); and/or

  - have moving objects blurred and one or more objects having no motion blurring in the photograph, with or without bokeh and/or selective focusing elements present.

The importance of expected outcomes for deciding on a micro-teach topic and overall planning of the session

As you can see, we have managed to differentiate expected outcomes by learner knowledge, experience or existing ability. This allows us to evaluate and review the planned resources to see whether or not they are adequate and likely to meet individual learner needs. Naturally, the estimation of such needs is not an exact science, since information or disclosure (especially of disability or particular learning difficulties) are likely to be limited or not sufficiently objective (i.e. audience members might over-estimate or under-estimate their abilities / aptitude).

Based on the information available, the expected outcomes and our own subject knowledge and experience, it seems as though we have a strong topic for a successful micro-teach (at least at the planning stage).

Reasonable adjustments and their treatment

Factors we have not yet considered as part of differentiation and meeting individual learner needs:

1. Learning difficulties

2. Disabilities

3. Medical conditions

Such factors may or may not apply. Two approaches can be adopted. The first is to formally request disclosure of any such conditions and record them. The second is to anticipate and embed these into the session. For instance, flash photography can be avoided, which could trigger an episode for those suffering from photosensitive epilepsy. A tripod could be available for individuals who have difficulty in maintaining a still composure or minimal hand movement. Any written notes could be in bullet points, succinct and supported by verbal instructions and related images, which should prove useful to those individuals who have dyslexia. Ideally, both approaches should be used and documented accordingly, with such records provided to the session observer at the beginning of the observation (assuming that all data protection protocols have been followed, i.e. explicit consent has been given by learners for such disclosure). This should look particularly good during a micro-teach delivered as part of a job interview and may be considered to be good practice. Naturally, for an interview situation, the first approach is unlikely, but a blank form can be provided, with notes about the approach that could be adopted, together with a risk analysis. The second approach is more likely to be considered to be good practice, since some disabilities and learning difficulties might be hidden or learners themselves might not know that they have such disabilities or learning difficulties. In relation to the Ofsted common inspection framework, this is likely to align with elements of embedding equality and diversity.

In relation to awarding organisations it is also likely to align with aspects of equality and diversity, as well as reasonable adjustments, while for the Award in Education and Training, it is relevant to the assessment criteria 3.1 and 3.2 of the unit entitled *Understanding Roles, Responsibilities and Relationships in Education and Training* and possibly also assessment criteria 1.4 and 2.1 of the unit entitled *Understanding Assessment in Education and Training*. However, you will need to explain the relevance of the approaches to those assessment criteria when completing the related assessment tasks (see further Appendix 1).

The next step is to consider devising a lesson plan.

Preparing a lesson plan

An effective lesson plan should outline 12 elements:

1. the topic, lecturer, venue and learner numbers;

2. the aims of the session;

3. The session objectives;

4. how each session objective is to be assessed;

5. cross reference to the awarding organisation assessment objectives / criteria being addressed;

6. a logical structure, such as a start, middle and end to the session;

7. activities undertaken by the lecturer and learners;

8. clear timings for each activity;

9. links to the previous and next sessions;

10. resources and learning materials being used;

11. differentiation strategies;

12. a self-evaluation section, to be completed by the lecturer at the end of the session, evaluating the extent to which the delivery matched the lesson plan.

The above is not an exhaustive list. Some learning providers might expect more, while others could expect less. Being thoroughly prepared is essential to success.

Lesson plan options

Prepare a lesson plan for the micro-teach only

Preparing a dedicated lesson plan for the micro-teach session might be appropriate, particularly for the Award in Education and Training. The key advantages of this approach are that the lesson plan is easy to follow and it should take less time to prepare than a full lesson plan. However, in a competitive job interview, it may not compare well to other candidates, many of whom may possess more experience than yourself and understand the importance of lesson planning and related documentation, especially if they have been formally observed in their previous workplace by a line manager or by an Ofsted inspector. The interview panel may prefer seeing an entire lesson plan so that they can place your micro-teach into context. If others have provided a full lesson plan, with a component that comprises a micro-teach element or a separate lesson plan for the micro-teach session and an overall session plan, then this might place you at a disadvantage, especially with any related follow-up questions during interview.

Prepare a lesson plan for the micro-teach and an overall lesson plan which includes the micro-teach component

From a lesson observer's point of view, this approach allows the observer to examine the micro-teach lesson plan and follow the delivery. After the session is delivered, the lesson observer can look at the overall lesson plan and examine the micro-teach in context (i.e. examine what you planned to do before introducing the micro-teach topic and following the micro-teach element). For instance, if you were asked at interview, how the session would develop after the micro-teach element, the full lesson plan would provide you with a clear guide for signposting your response.

The next few pages show a suggested lesson plan for this micro-teach session, together with annotations, analysis and places the micro-teach into context, cross-referencing other units of the course. An overall lesson plan is then produced for a complete session incorporating the micro-teach elements, with annotations for the full lesson plan.

Micro-teach lesson plan

Academic Year:	2014 - 2015	Prepared by:	Nabeel Zaidi
		Learning provider:	ETC

Course code: 001/2014		Course title: Award in Education and Training	
Room: 23	Duration: 26 minutes	Topic: Learning to photograph like a professional - bokeh and more	Class size: 6

Lesson Aim: *What do you hope to achieve in this lesson?*

1. Those new to digital photography will learn how to photograph with background blurring (bokeh)
2. Those with existing experience of digital photography (including using a DSLR camera) will learn how to photograph with background blurring and have extension activities, including use of selective focusing and adjusted shutter speeds.

Lesson Objectives: *By the end of the lesson **all** learners will be able to:*	**Assessment Strategies used to measure each objective**
1. **Use** a DSLR camera with a 50 mm f 1.8 lens to **create** a simple bokeh effect, using ambient light (and without using a flash)	1. Observation, questioning and photographic evidence
2. **Adjust** the bokeh effect, **using** basic techniques, such as moving the object in focus closer and further away.	2. Observation, questioning and photographic evidence
	3. Observation, photographic evidence and questioning during or after photographic composition (ensuring that the technique being applied is intentional rather than accidental)
Lesson Objectives: *By the end of the lesson **some** learners will be able to:*	
3. **Use** a DSLR camera with a 50 mm f 1.8 lens to **create** an effective bokeh effect, taking advantage of spot lighting for smoother bokeh and ensuring that the object in focus is sharply in focus	4. Observation (in particular, checking that the learner makes the manual adjustments to the aperture setting)
4. **Adjust** the lens aperture to **create** varying levels of blurring (e.g. use of f 1.8, f 2.8)	5. Observation, questioning and photographic evidence (preferably with more than one photograph of different objects being in focus)
5. **Use** selective focusing, with varying degrees of bokeh	6. Observation, questioning and photographic evidence.
6. Manually **adjust** the shutter speed to **create** a sense of motion, with one or more objects remaining still and in focus, while those moving experience motion blurring.	

18

Use of Study Support in Lesson: *e.g. How/when will Learner Support be used?*	Health and Safety: *matters to be addressed.*
• Advanced learners will provide peer support to beginners, where time permits. This is in addition to support provided by the person delivering the micro-teach • There were no requests for additional learning support during prior consultation with learners.	• No flash photography is to be used in this micro-teach • Tables and objects will be placed at a sufficient distance apart and will not obstruct walkways • Where tripods are used, these will not obstruct walkways and will not be left unattended by learners • There will be sufficient space allocated for taking photographs of moving subjects (for the purposes of creating motion blurring).
Equality and diversity • Learners have been consulted beforehand about individual learning needs, disabilities, learning difficulties and medical conditions that could affect their performance during this micro-teach. Reasonable adjustments have been made, as needed (a note of such adjustments is attached herewith) • Objects being used and learning materials are culturally sensitive or culturally neutral (e.g. no naked images of the human form are used).	**Other**

Timing	Content	Teaching methods	Learner activities	Assessment	Resources	Differentiation
Introduction / review						
10.00 - 10.02	Set out ground rules and outline lesson objectives.	Lecture and presentation.	Listen and ask questions where needed.	Verbal questioning to check understanding.	PowerPoint slides.	Embedded in the lesson objectives.

19

Timing	Content	Teaching methods	Learner activities	Assessment	Resources	Differentiation
Main content						
10.03 - 10.10	How to use a DSLR camera and appropriate lens to create bokeh.	Presentation, demonstration.	Take notes and observe. Advanced learners to share their experience.	Undirected and directed questions to check learning.	Photographs, short video clips.	Advanced learners share their experience of using a DSLR and basic bokeh techniques.
10.11 - 10.15	Using selective focus.	Presentation, demonstration.	As above.	As above.	As above.	Handouts with instructions on how to use selective focusing and different shutter speeds (for advanced users or those finishing early).
10.16 - 10.24	Taking photographs using one or more techniques.	Facilitating paired activities, providing verbal summative and formative feedback.	Taking photographs using one or more techniques.	Observation and photographic evidence. Multiple choice questions for those finishing early.	2 DSLR cameras with 50 mm f 1.8 lenses, 2 laptops, SD card reader.	
Summary / review						
10.25 - 10.26	Check learner progress against lesson objectives.	Lecture and question and answer.	Provide responses / feedback on the extent to which they believe the lesson objectives have been met.	Undirected and directed question and answer.	PowerPoint.	Advanced learners comment on the lesson objectives that apply to them.

Feedback from tutor and audience members / learners to the person delivering the micro-teach, who takes notes accordingly. If the session is videoed, together with the above feedback, a copy should be provided to the person delivering the micro-teach. These are to be used to inform evaluation and reflection.

Evaluation	Identify what went well in this session.	Identify what could be improved for the next time this session is.
	<ul><li>Session completed on time;</li><li>A range of evidence provided, demonstrating that the most of the lesson objectives had been met;</li><li>All learners were on task during the session;</li><li>Instructions were followed effectively during the photography part of the session.</li></ul>	<ul><li>Advanced learners were unable to take photographs using different shutter speeds, since they had limited time with the two cameras. At least 3 cameras are needed for a class of 6;</li><li>Some learners had over-estimated their ability to use DSLR cameras and needed additional support. In future, there should be more effective initial assessment, including testing learners' perceived ability to use a DSLR camera effectively.</li></ul>

Analysis of the micro-teach lesson plan

Lesson Aim: *What do you hope to achieve in this lesson?*

1. Those new to digital photography will learn how to photograph with background blurring (bokeh)
2. Those with existing experience of digital photography (including using a DSLR camera) will learn how to photograph with background blurring and have extension activities, including use of selective focusing and adjusted shutter speeds.

This outlines the overall purpose of the lesson, with an outline of what learning will take place.

The observations should be accompanied with brief notes as evidence of checking learning.

Questions should be undirected and directed, with differing levels of difficulty and follow-up (i.e. they should be differentiated).

Lesson Objectives: *By the end of the lesson **all** learners will be able to:*

1. **Use** a DSLR camera with a 50 mm f 1.8 lens to **create** a simple bokeh effect, using ambient light (and without using a flash)
2. **Adjust** the bokeh effect, **using** basic techniques, such as moving the object in focus closer and further away.

Lesson Objectives: *By the end of the lesson **some** learners will be able to:*

3. **Use** a DSLR camera with a 50 mm f 1.8 lens to **create** an effective bokeh effect, taking advantage of spot lighting for smoother bokeh and ensuring that the object in focus is sharply in focus
4. **Adjust** the lens aperture to **create** varying levels of blurring (e.g. use of f 1.8, f 2.8)
5. **Use** selective focusing, with varying degrees of bokeh
6. Manually **adjust** the shutter speed to **create** a sense of motion, with one or more objects remaining still and in focus, while those moving experience motion blurring.

Assessment Strategies used to measure each objective

1. Observation, questioning and photographic evidence
2. Observation, questioning and photographic evidence
3. Observation, photographic evidence and questioning during or after photographic composition (ensuring that the technique being applied is intentional rather than accidental)
4. Observation (in particular, checking that the learner makes the manual adjustments to the aperture setting)
5. Observation, questioning and photographic evidence (preferably with more than one photograph of different objects being in focus)
6. Observation, questioning and photographic evidence.

These are command verbs, similar to those one would expect to see in unit assessment criteria and of a course. The use of command verbs clarifies the scope of the task to be performed and have of a specific meaning. Where a lesson is being delivered and is aligned to one or more unit assessment criteria, the command verbs should align to some or most of the lesson objectives. For instance if the assessment criteria being targeted during the lesson requires a learner to 'explain' a concept, then teaching them to 'identify' the concept is not sufficient, since the two mean very different things.

The combination of observation, questioning and photographic evidence ensures effective triangulation of evidence. For instance, observation provides assurance that the learner is carrying out the task by themselves or with limited support, while questioning checks that the learner understands what they are doing and that the photographic evidence was not achieved by accident or luck.

Use of Study Support in Lesson: *e.g. How/when will Learner Support be used?*
- Advanced learners will provide peer support to beginners, where time permits. This is in addition to support provided by the person delivering the micro-teach
- There were no requests for additional learning support during prior consultation with learners.

Equality and diversity
- Learners have been consulted beforehand about individual learning needs, disabilities, learning difficulties and medical conditions that could affect their performance during this micro-teach. Reasonable adjustments have been made, as needed (a note of such adjustments is attached herewith)
- Objects being used and learning materials are culturally sensitive or culturally neutral (e.g. no naked images of the human form are used).

Any requests for additional learning support should be noted and used to inform planning and delivery strategies.

Health and Safety: *matters to be addressed.*
- No flash photography is to be used in this micro-teach
- Tables and objects will be placed at a sufficient distance apart and will not obstruct walkways
- Where tripods are used, these will not obstruct walkways and will not be left unattended by learners
- There will be sufficient space allocated for taking photographs of moving subjects (for the purposes of creating motion blurring).

Other

This reduces the risk to learners with photosensitive epilepsy.

| Record of reasonable adjustments | | | |

Learner's name	Details of disclosed disability, learning difficulty or medical condition requiring reasonable adjustment(s)	Details of authorisation given, otherwise leave blank.	Details of reasonable adjustments made and agreed with the learner.
Andy J. Murray	Lateral epicondylitis ('tennis elbow'). Symptoms: pain at the elbow when gripping something or using a twisting motion.	N/A	Additional tripod to be provided, together with a DSLR camera remote. This should minimise arm movement and ensure the camera remains stable when taking photographs. The learner has agreed to this adjustment. This adjustment does not place the learner at an advantage to other learners during the assessment. The sharper image due to the tripod and remote will be taken into account, but given that it is a low light lens, with image stabilisation, the increase in sharpness is likely to be nominal.

Evaluation	Identify what went well in this session.	Identify what could be improved for the next time this session is.
	• Session completed on time; • A range of evidence provided, demonstrating that the most of the lesson objectives had been met; • All learners were on task during the session; • Instructions were followed effectively during the photography part of the session.	• Advanced learners were unable to take photographs using different shutter speeds, since they had limited time with the two cameras. At least 3 cameras are needed for a class of 6; • Some learners had over-estimated their ability to use DSLR cameras and needed additional support. In future, there should be more effective initial assessment, including testing learners' perceived ability to use a DSLR camera effectively.

What will the initial assessment include? How will its effectiveness be evaluated? Will it be able to identify where learners have under-estimated their ability to use a DSLR camera? How much time and resources will be committed to undertaking the initial assessment? Could the time expended on the initial assessment be better utilised during an extended micro-teach session (especially if support structures, extension activities and additional resources are in place)? Teaching, learning and assessment strategies have time, cost and resourcing implications and a good lecturer will seek to strike an appropriate balance - one which maximises learning and has the interests of the learner at its heart.

Ideally, this should not have occurred. What went wrong during the resourcing stage? What lessons, if any, can be learnt for the future? Will 3 cameras be enough? How is this figure arrived at? Should the micro-teach have had a greater focus on fewer techniques and more time allocated to taking photographs? In the long run, being self critical and reflective about an ineffective delivery is as important as having a good delivery. Sometimes the lessons learnt from mistakes are more profound than the lessons learnt from a smooth delivery. The evaluation of the micro-teach should be detailed and balanced. There are instances, however, where there is virtually no room for error, most notably when delivering a session to paying delegates. In such cases a dry run of the delivery and peer feedback is advisable, time and resources permitting.

<u>General note</u>

Individuals reflecting on their micro-teach often focus on the areas for improvement / development rather than the elements that went well and why they went well. While there should be priority given to areas for development, strengths, good practice or good features in a session should not be ignored. In the regime of continuous improvement across the further education sector, one needs to prioritise areas for development, but also consider strategies to secure continued good practice or good features in a session and work towards enhancement (i.e. in basic terms, this would look at making something good even better). After all, inspections, reviews and visits from awarding organisations examine progress made since the last visit, including follow-up on actions, recommendations and in many cases areas of good practice. Therefore any reflection and development plan should look at areas for development and how these can be addressed, good practice and how to ensure it continues and can be enhanced (i.e. made even better). This form of evaluation should prove to be effective in informing continuous improvement and align with departmental and learning provider expectations and quality improvement plans (QIP) and related strategies.

During an interview for a teaching or training related position, the micro-teach could last anything from 5 to 15 minutes. It could be delivered to teaching staff, managers, the interview panel or learners, with a manager observing and feeding back to the interview panel.

Important features of the micro-teach, including the lesson plan, are likely to be:

- Effective time keeping in line with the time frame stated in the lesson plan;

- Teaching, learning and assessment strategies;

- Differentiation strategies;

- Consideration of equality and diversity;

- Consideration of reasonable adjustments;

- The learning materials and resources used;

- Use of ICT / ILT;

- Planned learner engagement and learner-centred approaches, with greater emphasis on learning than teaching;

- Strategies to maximise learner engagement, participation and achievement;

- The structure, logical progression and pace of the session;

- Ensuring that learner evidence generated is authentic, reliable and robust (this is particularly relevant for internally assessed programmes).

The more that a micro-teach lesson plan and associated documentation can include and anticipate from the list above, the easier it becomes to answer questions related to the above points.

The lesson plan in the preceding pages is fully differentiated by ability and takes account of prior learning and experience, it is focused on learning, with active participation of all learners, it meets individual learner needs, makes and records reasonable adjustments and takes account of equality and diversity, the lesson objectives are clearly defined and cross referenced to robust and triangulated assessment strategies that ensure the learner work is authentic (i.e. their own), reliable and that learners fully understand what they are doing, there is appropriate and effective use of ICT / ILT, with the incorporation of PowerPoint, digital images, You Tube clips and laptops, and the session is learner-centred (i.e. there is a clear focus on learning, with hands-on experience of photographic techniques). The lesson plan includes opportunities for the lecturer to evaluate and reflect on the effectiveness of the session, with an emphasis on informing continuous improvement. Therefore, the lesson plan has already met most of the bullet points listed above before delivery takes place.

Course related considerations for the micro-teach

Self-evaluation and reflection are important characteristics of effective teaching practice. A good starting point is to critically evaluate the lesson plan against the most relevant learning outcomes and assessment criteria of the unit entitled *Understanding and Using Inclusive Teaching and Learning Approaches in Education and Training*. The relevant learning outcome and assessment criteria are as follows:

Learning Outcome 3: "Be able to plan inclusive teaching and learning."

Assessment Criterion 3.1: "Devise an inclusive teaching and learning plan."

Assessment Criterion 3.2: "Justify own selection of teaching and learning approaches, resources and assessment methods in relation to meeting individual learner needs."

In terms of the lesson plan, we will need to evaluate it against assessment criterion (AC) 3.1. We then need to look at a detailed written justification for AC 3.2, based on the lesson plan and teaching, learning and assessment methods / approaches and fitness for purpose of the selected resources.

Assessment Criterion 3.1: "Devise an inclusive teaching and learning plan."

The following points should support inclusive learning:

- The lesson aims and objects are clearly defined and communicated (see associated PowerPoint slides later in this book);
- There is a logical structure to the session;
- Timings are appropriate for teaching, learning and assessment and allow for learner questions / queries to be raised at any point during the lesson and are encouraged;
- A variety of teaching, learning and assessment strategies are employed;
- There are support considerations in place;
- Reasonable adjustments have been made;
- Equality and diversity and health and safety have been considered, as well as medical conditions / disability;
- Differentiation strategies and supporting resources are in place, with clear learning outcomes for different groups of learners, based on ability, prior knowledge and experience and just in case they finish the allotted tasks early;
- A range of learning styles are included;
- Learning resources and the approach adopted are engaging and focus on individual and group participation;
- Visual aids, such as photographs and video clips provide exemplars of the output that is expected and are comparable to the camera and lens being used (i.e. some of the photographs have been taken using the same camera and lens, so many of the displayed results are likely to be achieved;
- There are opportunities for formative feedback and guidance during the learning activities;
- Peer support is encouraged.

Assessment Criterion 3.2: "Justify own selection of teaching and learning approaches, resources and assessment methods in relation to meeting individual learner needs."

The table below outlines and justifies the teaching and learning approaches, resources used and assessment methods employed.

Approach	Justification
TEACHING	
Lecture	Provides an opportunity to disseminate significant information in a timely manner.
Question and answer	Quick checks on learning. An opportunity to engage all learners through undirected and directed questions. Learners can also ask questions, thereby increasing interaction.
Presentation	Use of PowerPoint, with multimedia content should appeal to learners, focus on a range of learning styles and provide an effective structure for delivery.
Demonstration	Effective in providing practical explanation on how to use the camera and lens. Should appeal to visual and kinaesthetic learners.
Facilitating learning activities	Ensures learning is taking place within an effective structure, at an appropriate pace and that learners remain on task during the activities.
Summative and formative feedback	Provide a check on whether learners are completing the task correctly or answering questions correctly and what they need to do next to improve. Feedback is instant, thereby allowing learners to make improvements immediately and potentially increasing their motivation.
LEARNING	
Making or taking notes	These act as an aide memoir and should appeal to learners with a preference for reading and writing.
Observing demonstrations	Given that the topic is practical in nature and learners are expected to undertake equivalent practical tasks, this approach should prove effective.

Approach	Justification
LEARNING continued	
Peers share their experience of photography	Peer-to-peer sharing of photographic techniques should be motivational, increase opportunities for discussion, engagement and raise social interaction.
Providing or receiving peer support during learning activities	This will provide one peer the opportunity and experience of teaching, while the other peer will learn, freeing up some time for the person delivering the micro-teach to observe, facilitate and provide feedback. This activity is also related to peer assessment, which is considered in another AET unit.
Taking photographs	"Learning by doing" should appeal to kinaesthetic learners and is a natural part of the topic.
RESOURCES	
2 DSLR cropped frame cameras	These are standard professional entry level cameras and are capable of producing bokeh results with appropriate lenses. Mirrorless cameras do exist, but the choice of dedicated lenses is limited and the features are less extensive. Two cameras were considered to be sufficient for a group of six learners.
50 mm f 1.8 prime lens	A prime lens was selected since it has superior image capabilities when compared to most zoom lenses and is almost comparable to Canon L-series lenses (these are professional grade lenses). The Canon version is low cost, with excellent results. F 1.8 is a good entry point for generating effective bokeh images. F 1.2 and f 1.4 are professionally accepted, but mainly for portrait photography and work better with a full frame camera and are far more expensive lenses.
Tripod	This is essential for taking photographs with adjusted shutter speeds and for the planned reasonable adjustment for one of the learners.

Approach	Justification
RESOURCES continued	
2 laptops, 4 SD cards and 2 SD card readers	Learners can alternate between taking photographs and viewing them on the laptops. SD card readers are needed in order to do so, as are 4 SD cards (2 in use in the cameras and two in the laptops).
Exemplar photographs	Provide learners with an example of the finished product so that they are clear about the outcome of using the various photographic techniques.
You Tube video clips	Learners can see how amateurs and professionals use the range of techniques being taught. It adds variety, professional context and in settings that make the topic aspirational and engaging.
Instructional handouts for extension tasks (adjusted shutter speeds)	Extension activities provide challenge, and instructions should reduce some of the demands on the time of the person delivering the micro-teach. They can focus on supporting and observing other learners.
Tables and objects	These are needed for depth of field / creating varying bokeh effects.
ASSESSMENT METHODS	
Using up to three forms of assessment methods for triangulation	A combination of assessment methods have been used to ensure authenticity and reliability of the photographs produced and to check that learners understand the techniques they are applying and why.
Observation	This ensures the learner work is authentic and creates opportunities to provide guidance and feedback, as needed.
Question and answer	This checks learning and understanding, identifying possible gaps that require guidance, support and developmental / formative feedback.
Photographs	Evidence of outcome and can be used for summative and formative feedback.

Justifying teaching and learning approaches, resources used and assessment methods should prove useful in quality assuring your lesson plan. For instance, while drafting the justification, I found myself updating the lesson plan, since there were some resourcing gaps, such as the number of SD cards needed. I had only accounted for two SD cards in my resourcing list initially. Drafting the justification made me realise that four SD cards would be needed. Had I not undertaken the justification and only resourced for two SD cards, it is likely to have adversely impacted on the learning activity part of the micro-teach session, leading to more learners waiting around to use the equipment or copy over SD card content.

With resource intensive practical lessons, any minor errors or miscalculations in logistics and resourcing can have a dramatic effect on the timing and quality of the lesson and the learner experience. If the lesson is being formally observed by a line manager, it could result in a reduction of lesson observation grades. A lesson could quite easily go from being 'good' (grade 2) to 'requires improvement' (grade 3) (assuming an Ofsted aligned lesson observation). The importance of preparation and planning should not be under-estimated.

The micro-teach in the context of the rest of the course units and particular assessment criteria

There is a degree of overlap between planning and delivery of the micro-teach and other units of the Award in Education and Training. Understanding the interconnections at the beginning of the course and before your planning and delivery of the micro-teach should benefit both the quality of your micro-teach preparation and delivery as well as the responses you provide for assessments on other units. Some of the key elements are considered below.

Unit: Understanding Roles, Responsibilities and Relationships in Education and Training

Assessment criterion 1.2: "Summarise key aspects of legislation, regulatory requirements and codes of practice relating to own role and responsibilities."

In this lesson plan, aspects of equality and diversity and health and safety have been considered and applied appropriately. Reading relevant elements of the Equality Act 2010 and/or related guidance and the Health and Safety at Work etc. Act 1974 and/or related guidance would provide some of the background needed to apply them to the micro-teach preparation and delivery. Meanwhile, familiarising oneself with awarding organisation expectations for making reasonable adjustments would assist in acceptable ideas and underpinning principles of identifying, seeking permission for (where relevant), applying and recording such adjustments.

Assume that the micro-teach has been delivered as part of a job interview and the interview panel ask the question about how equality and diversity can be embedded in the curriculum. A starting point would be to consider opportunities for making reasonable adjustments to assessments without compromising the quality, validity and reliability of the assessment. This is where an understanding of the equality and diversity legislation, related guidance and awarding organisation requirements would prove useful in formulating an effective response. If supporting examples related to a subject specialism can be applied that should result in a more persuasive response.

Assessment criterion 1.3: "Explain ways to promote equality and value diversity."

An example of promoting equality can be seen in the lesson plan, with reasonable adjustments being made to take account of medical conditions and anticipate the impact of flash photography, if used, for learners with photosensitive epilepsy. There is some aspect of valuing diversity in the form of 'internationalising the curriculum'. For instance, the video clips feature a range of presenters from different racial backgrounds and based in different countries. This 'internationalises' the use of photographic techniques, providing examples of how photography is used in different contexts. The images used are culturally sensitive, ensuring there is no unnecessary nudity, and individuals are dressed modestly. This takes account of cultural and religious sensitivity.

Assessment criterion 1.4: "Explain why it is important to identify and meet individual learner needs."

The session has been differentiated and includes recognition of prior learning and experience. In fact, the session and resources have been adjusted based on this. Why is this important? You should now be in a better position to respond to this type of question, based on the lesson plan just prepared. Learners are also encouraged to share their experience and be actively involved, which is another element of assessment criterion 1.4. Depending on the sequence the units are delivered in and assessments completed, you can benefit from reflecting on aspects of your micro-teach and including supporting examples from it. This should prove useful for interview preparation for a teaching or training role, because you can outline the benefits of responding to individual learner needs and then demonstrate how you responded to such needs during your micro-teach, as part of the Award in Education and Training course.

Assessment criterion 2.1: "Explain ways to maintain a safe and supportive learning environment."

The lesson plan makes reference to health and safety and takes certain aspects into account. Learner support has also been considered.

Assessment criterion 2.2: "Explain why it is important to promote appropriate behaviour and respect for others."

Encouraging peer working and support, as in this micro-teach, is one means of achieving respect for others.

Assessment criterion 3.1: "Explain how the teaching role involves working with other professionals."

In further education colleges and medium sized learning providers there are often dedicated staff and/or departments providing additional learning support. Where learners are known to have learning difficulties additional support can be arranged. Where disabilities or learning difficulties require reasonable adjustments to be made to assessments (e.g. extra time in examinations), then the examinations officer or department need to ensure that any additional time is in line with awarding organisation guidelines. This is important to know and explain during a teaching related job interview. For instance, if you

state that you would make reasonable adjustments in a session, but do not recognise that you may need to liaise with other professionals within the learning provider and perhaps the awarding organisation to do so then it weakens the quality of your response. The reasonable adjustment made in this micro-teach was minimal and not likely to advantage the learner with the medical condition. A tripod was to be provided for some learners in any case. However, some types of reasonable adjustment require line manager and/or examination officer or awarding organisation approval.

Unit: Understanding and Using Inclusive Teaching and Learning Approaches in Education and Training

In addition to the micro-teach related assessment criteria in the above unit, the assessment criterion stated below is also relevant to the micro-teach.

Assessment criterion 2.4: "Summarise ways to establish ground rules with learners."

In relation to the micro-teach session, ground rules can be established in the following ways:

- A brief outline of housekeeping (i.e. where the toilets are located, what to do in the event of a fire drill or real fire, who to contact in relation to first aid, the schedule/timing for the lesson);
- Guidance as to when questions can be asked during or after the delivery of the presentation element of the micro-teach;
- Etiquette as to asking questions (e.g. raising one's hand, not interrupting another learner who is asking a question);
- How the photographic equipment is to be used and shared between learners;
- The extent and nature of any peer support to be given during the session;
- Behaviour and conduct expected during the session;
- Timing, nature and style of any feedback given by learners to the person delivering the micro-teach at the end of the session.

In any professional training delivery, some of the above elements would be present, especially the first two bullet points. For a micro-teach in an job interview, housekeeping is less likely to be relevant, since it is assumed that this has already taken place previously (i.e. a snapshot is being taken of part of the session, unless otherwise indicated) although the second and third bullet points would normally be appropriate.

Unit: Understanding Assessment in Education and Training

Assessment criterion 1.3: "Compare the strengths and limitations of different assessment methods in relation to meeting individual learner needs."

The justifications for the assessment methods used in the micro-teach can support part of your response for the above assessment criteria and vice versa, depending on which unit you complete first. The choice of assessment methods might be relevant to questions in an interview. What is important here is that there is a clear rationale and justification for selecting the assessment methods and that they are suitable for the target audience, taking full account of their individual needs.

Assessment criterion 1.4: "Explain how different assessment methods can be adapted to meet individual learner needs."

This has been demonstrated to an extent in the micro-teach preparation, with differentiated activities and the reasonable adjustment that has been applied. In an interview situation, you need to be aware of the Equality Act 2010 and associated guidance, related expectations of inspection and review bodies (e.g. Ofsted, ISI, BAC, QAA) and awarding organisation guidance on reasonable adjustments from the awarding organisation and possibly JCQ, which regulates the conduct of examinations across the UK.[1]

Assessment criterion 2.1: "Explain why it is important to involve learners and others in the assessment process."

Earlier in this textbook, it was recommended that your target audience for the micro-teach were consulted about the topic area and their individual

learning needs prior to confirming the topic of your micro-teach. In an interview situation, you are not likely to be able to undertake this kind of activity. However, if you were asked a question on how learners could be involved in the assessment process, your response could cover the following aspects:

- Consultation as to preferred assessment methods;
- Discussion about preferred learning styles, which could inform the assessment practice and adjustments thereto;
- Sharing with learners the assessment criteria and how they are going to be assessed;
- Being clear about the assessment that will take place in the lesson and what is expected of them, including sharing exemplar materials of completed assessments as a sample (we have done this in the current micro-teach example);
- Providing opportunities to learners to feedback on their experience of teaching, learning and assessment practices at the learning provider.

Another aspect, which is covered in part in this micro-teach example, is concerning what steps to take to ensure that the evidence generated from assessment is valid, authentic, reliable and robust. Triangulation, as already discussed earlier, would be relevant here. If the interview is for a position delivering internally assessed programmes, questions could focus on working with colleagues and line managers to standardise, double mark (normally relevant in higher education), internally verify and otherwise quality assure the assessments.

Assessment criterion 2.2: "Explain the role and use of peer- and self-assessment in the assessment process."

Although the micro-teach example provided has not built-in self or peer assessment (mainly due to time constraints), it is something that can be considered in the context of a full lesson plan (see example provided later on in this textbook). In relation to interviews, especially for certain internally assessed qualifications, independent learning is becoming increasingly important. How would you develop independent learners? is a possible interview question for some learning providers. Part of the response could focus on introducing or embedding

---

[1] See: http://www.jcq.org.uk/

self and peer assessments into lessons and assessments.

Assessment criterion 3.2: "Explain how constructive feedback contributes to the assessment process."

In the micro-teach example provided, there are opportunities set aside for constructive feedback to learners during the learning activities and for learners to provide constructive feedback on the micro-teach itself. Referring to an interview situation, the key elements about feedback are likely to be as follows:

- What type and extent of feedback is expected by awarding organisations?
- Is the feedback in an appropriate format for learners relative to their individual learning needs and is it timely?
- Is summative feedback detailed?
- Is formative feedback sufficiently developmental (e.g. does it provide details of next steps for improvement or enhancement and are developmental targets SMART - specific, measurable, achievable, realistic and time bound)?
- How do you ensure that feedback is constructive and motivates learners to achieve?

Further reading and research for the course, interview preparation and professional development

- *Achieving your Award in Education and Training: The Comprehensive Course Companion (Special Edition)* by Nabeel Zaidi
- The latest inspection, accreditation and review frameworks, depending on the learning provider concerned (see Ofsted[1], ISI[2], BAC[3], QAA[4]), in particular any aspects focusing on teaching, learning, assessment and quality assurance.
- Publications by Geoff Petty.[5]
- Presentation related textbooks by experts in the field (e.g. *Presentation Zen* by Gar Reynolds)
- *Professional Standards for Teachers and Trainers in Education and Training - England*[6]

- For sector developments refer to the following:
  - The Education and Training Foundation[7]
  - TES[8]
  - THES[9]
  - BIS[10]
  - AOC[11]
  - UCU[12]

The lesson plan and related documentation for a full session and its relevance to a job interview

In practice, a lesson plan for a full session would be linked to a scheme of work and have links to the previous and next session. During a lesson observation, which can last up to an hour (or in some cases for the entire session, depending on the learning provider's policies and procedures), the observer would normally expect to see a scheme of work, the lesson plan for the session, a register of learners enrolled on the programme, records of learner progress (e.g. task, unit and/or module tracking sheets) and a copy of the learning materials, PowerPoint slides and handouts for the session. In order to ensure completeness, a sample of assessed learner work, with summative and formative feedback, a pen portrait[13], individual learning plans (ILP's)[14] and the awarding organisation unit and qualification specifications can also be supplied. Being familiar with these documents, their purpose and application should assist in answering some questions during an interview for a teaching or training position. A sample annotated lesson plan is provided on the next few pages.

---

[6] http://www.et-foundation.co.uk/wp-content/uploads/2014/05/4991-Prof-standards-A4_4-2.pdf
[7] http://www.et-foundation.co.uk/
[8] https://www.tes.co.uk/
[9] https://www.timeshighereducation.co.uk/
[10] https://www.gov.uk/government/organisations/department-for-business-innovation-skills
[11] http://www.aoc.co.uk/
[12] http://www.ucu.org.uk/
[13] A pen portrait can include learner information, such as attendance rates, additional support needs, target minimum grades, latest predicted grades based on performance to date and any other relevant comments or information.
[14] ILP's monitor and review learner progress on a regular basis (sometimes on a weekly basis for short courses or termly for longer courses) and set achievement and performance targets that learners should be meeting.

---

[1] https://www.gov.uk/government/organisations/ofsted
[2] http://www.educationaloversight.co.uk/home/
[3] http://www.the-bac.org/
[4] http://www.qaa.ac.uk/en
[5] http://geoffpetty.com/

Lesson plan (full lesson)

Academic Year: 2014 - 2015

Prepared by: Nabeel Zaidi

Learning provider: ETC

Course code: 012/2014		Course title: Practical Photography	
Room: 23	Duration: 90 minutes	Topic: Understanding and creating bokeh effects using different techniques	Class size: 6

Lesson Aim: *What do you hope to achieve in this lesson?*

1. All learners will be introduced to the benefits of using prime lenses, with a large aperture size and their impact on depth of field
2. Those new to digital photography will learn how to photograph with background blurring (bokeh)
3. Those with existing experience of digital photography (including using a DSLR camera) will learn how to photograph with background blurring and have extension activities, including use of selective focusing and adjusted shutter speeds.

Lesson Objectives: *By the end of the lesson all learners will be able to:*	**Assessment Strategies used to measure each objective**
1. **Explain** the benefits of using a prime lens with a large aperture size 2. **Outline** the impact of using a large aperture size (i.e. with small f-stops, from f 1.2 to f 2.8) on depth of field 3. **Use** a DSLR camera with a 50 mm f 1.8 lens to **create** a simple bokeh effect, using ambient light (and without using a flash) 4. **Adjust** the bokeh effect, **using** basic techniques, such as moving the object in focus closer and further away. **Lesson Objectives:** *By the end of the lesson **some** learners will be able to:* 5. Provide a **detailed explanation**, with supporting examples, of the benefits of using prime lenses with a large aperture size 6. **Explain** the impact of using a large aperture size (i.e. with small f-stops, from f 1.2 to f 2.8) on depth of field	1. Written response under timed conditions, with peer assessment against suggested response 2. Matching exercise, with a series of statements and photographs. Learners are required to match the correct statement to the corresponding photograph, with self-assessment marked against correct response to matches 3. Observation, questioning and photographic evidence 4. Observation, questioning and photographic evidence 5. Alternative written response under timed conditions (i.e. there are two tasks, one for beginner level photographers and another for experienced photographers. Learners select the most appropriate task for them) 6. Alternative written response under timed conditions (i.e. there are two tasks, one for beginner level photographers (with the command verb 'outline') and another for experienced photographers (with the command verb 'explain'). Learners select the most appropriate task for them)

7. **Use** a DSLR camera with a 50 mm f 1.8 lens to **create** an effective bokeh effect, taking advantage of spot lighting for smoother bokeh and ensuring that the object in focus is sharply in focus
8. **Adjust** the lens aperture to **create** varying levels of blurring (e.g. use of f 1.8, f 2.8)
9. **Use** selective focusing, with varying degrees of bokeh
10. Manually **adjust** the shutter speed to **create** a sense of motion, with one or more objects remaining still and in focus, while those moving experience motion blurring.

7. Observation, photographic evidence and questioning during or after photographic composition (ensuring that the technique being applied is intentional rather than accidental)
8. Observation (in particular, checking that the learner makes the manual adjustments to the aperture setting)
9. Observation, questioning and photographic evidence (preferably with more than one photograph of different objects being in focus)
10. Observation, questioning and photographic evidence.

Generic matters to be addressed

Health and Safety: *matters to be addressed.*
- No flash photography is to be used in this session
- Tables and objects will be placed at a sufficient distance apart and will not obstruct walkways
- Where tripods are used, these will not obstruct walkways and will not be left unattended by learners
- There will be sufficient space allocated for taking photographs of moving subjects (for the purposes of creating motion blurring).

Use of Study Support in Lesson: *e.g. How/when will Learner Support be used?*
- Advanced learners will provide peer support to beginners, where time permits. This is in addition to support provided by the lecturer
- One learner has severe dyslexia, so may need some assistance with interpreting the written tasks or can provide a verbal explanation to clarify a written response provided.

Equality and diversity
- A pen portrait and records exist of individual learning needs, disabilities, learning difficulties and medical conditions that could affect their performance during this session. Reasonable adjustments have been made, as needed (a note of such adjustments is attached herewith)
- Objects being used and learning materials are culturally sensitive or culturally neutral (e.g. no naked images of the human form are used).

Other

Timing	Content	Teaching methods	Learner activities	Assessment	Resources	Differentiation
Introduction / review						
10.00 - 10.05	Brief recap of key points from previous lesson. Set out ground rules and outline lesson objectives.	Lecture and presentation.	Listen and ask questions where needed.	Verbal questioning to check understanding.	PowerPoint slides.	Embedded in the lesson objectives.

Timing	Content	Teaching methods	Learner activities	Assessment	Resources	Differentiation
Main content						
10.06 - 10.35	The characteristics and key benefits of using a prime lens with a large aperture.	Presentation and discussion.	Take notes, view a selection of photographs on screen and in handouts.	Written, with peer assessment.	Photographs on PowerPoint and in handouts, written exercise.	Different written tasks for beginners and those with experience of photography.
10.36 - 11.00	Large aperture prime lenses and relationship with depth of field.	Presentation and discussion.	Question and answer and discussion.	Matching exercise, with self assessment.	Photographs and statements for matching exercise.	Matching exercise, with varying degrees of difficulty, suitable for beginners and advanced users.
11.01 - 11.08	How to use a DSLR camera and appropriate lens to create bokeh.	Presentation, demonstration.	Take notes and observe. Advanced learners to share their experience.	Undirected and directed questions to check learning.	Photographs, short video clips.	Advanced learners share their experience of using a DSLR and basic bokeh techniques.
11.09 - 11.13	Using selective focus.	Presentation, demonstration.	As above.	As above.	As above.	Handouts with instructions on how to use selective focusing and different shutter speeds (for advanced users or those finishing early).
11.14 - 11.22	Taking photographs using one or more techniques.	Facilitating paired activities, providing verbal summative and formative feedback.	Taking photographs using one or more techniques.	Observation and photographic evidence. Multiple choice questions for those finishing early.	2 DSLR cameras with 50 mm f 1.8 lenses, 2 laptops, SD card reader.	
Summary / review						
11.23 - 11.30	Check learner progress against lesson objectives. Outline of topics to be covered in the next session.	Lecture and question and answer.	Provide responses / feedback on the extent to which they believe the lesson objectives have been met. Take notes on advanced reading for next session.	Undirected and directed question and answer.	PowerPoint.	Advanced learners comment on the lesson objectives that apply to them.

Evaluation	Identify what went well in this session.	Identify what could be improved for the next time this session is.
	• Session completed on time; • Overall, differentiated activities worked effectively, with learners of all abilities being fully engaged and sufficiently challenged; • A range of evidence provided, demonstrating that most of the lesson objectives had been met; • All learners were on task during the session; • Instructions were followed effectively during the photography part of the session.	• The matching activity requires more examples of photographs and statements, since one learners completed the exercise early; • Advanced learners were unable to take photographs using different shutter speeds, since they had limited time with the two cameras. At least 3 cameras are needed for a class of 6; • Some learners had over-estimated their ability to use DSLR cameras and needed additional support. In future, there should be more effective initial assessment, including testing learners' perceived ability to use a DSLR camera effectively.

<u>Key</u>

Red text represents the original
micro-teach lesson plan content.

Command verbs used in the lesson plan	Approximate meaning
Adjust	Make changes to.
Explain	Make something clear to someone by describing or revealing relevant information in more detail.
Outline	Identify accurately and describe clearly the main points.
Use	Apply.

Use of Study Support in Lesson: *e.g. How/when will Learner Support be used?*

- Advanced learners will provide peer support to beginners, where time permits. This is in addition to support provided by the lecturer
- One learner has severe dyslexia, so may need some assistance with interpreting the written tasks or can provide a verbal explanation to clarify a written response provided.

Health and Safety: *matters to be addressed.*

- No flash photography is to be used in this session
- Tables and objects will be placed at a sufficient distance apart and will not obstruct walkways
- Where tripods are used, these will not obstruct walkways and will not be left unattended by learners
- There will be sufficient space allocated for taking photographs of moving subjects (for the purposes of creating motion blurring).

Equality and diversity

- A pen portrait and records exist of individual learning needs, disabilities, learning difficulties and medical conditions that could affect their performance during this session. Reasonable adjustments have been made, as needed (a note of such adjustments is attached herewith)
- Objects being used and learning materials are culturally sensitive or culturally neutral (e.g. no naked images of the human form are used).

Other

Record of reasonable adjustments

Learner's name	Details of disclosed disability, learning difficulty or medical condition requiring reasonable adjustment(s)	Details of authorisation given, otherwise leave blank.	Details of reasonable adjustments made and agreed with the learner.
Andy J. Murray	Lateral epicondylitis ('tennis elbow'). Symptoms: pain at the elbow when gripping something or using a twisting motion.	N/A	Additional tripod to be provided, together with a DSLR camera remote. This should minimise arm movement and ensure the camera remains stable when taking photographs. The learner has agreed to this adjustment. This adjustment does not place the learner at an advantage to other learners during the assessment. The sharper image due to the tripod and remote will be taken into account, but given that it is a low light lens, with image stabilisation, the increase in sharpness is likely to be nominal.
Mandy Mann	Severe dyslexia (supporting evidence provided), which is likely to hinder full interpretation of written tasks and ability to provide an effective written task.	Authorisation provided by exams department and the awarding organisation.	Provide one-to-one support. Make available an audio recording device to record learner responses to written tasks as an alternative to or in addition to written responses.

Command verbs

Awarding organisations use command verbs for each of the assessment criteria in a unit and when setting assessment or examination tasks. Each command verb has a different meaning, which affects the quantity, quality and complexity of the evidence that is to be generated.

This has profound implications for planning a micro-teach and a full lesson. Some of these implications are considered below.

Quantity and complexity of evidence to be generated

The evidence required for the command verbs 'list' and 'explain' is normally shorter and less complex than the evidence required for the command verbs 'analyse' and 'evaluate'. Sequencing of command verbs is also important in a session, so that the command verbs and evidence generated act as a 'building block' to learning. Here is a simple example:

Task 1: **"State** four characteristics of a recession"

Task 2: **"Explain** how an individual might respond to a recession"

Task 3: **"Analyse** the likely impact on a small business of a recession"

The level of difficulty in the above tasks increases gradually, with 'state' being the easiest to respond to and 'analyse' being the most challenging. In a differentiated lesson, all learners are likely to be able to answer the first two tasks, while most, but not all, may be able to answer the last task.

Some might need more time in the current session or a subsequent session and/or an additional workshop in order to provide an effective response to the last task. Command verbs also have implications for the duration of a micro-teach.

Duration of a micro-teach

The shorter the micro-teach, the more likely it is that 'lower order' thinking skills will be required, which affects the command verbs selected.[1] Therefore, for a job interview with a ten minutes micro-teach, candidates are more likely to be asked to 'explain' a concept, principle or theory, rather than to 'analyse' it. Analysis is a lot more involved, necessitating greater input and in turn requiring more session time to deliver.

Strategic considerations

Effective use of command verbs in a micro-teach is likely to contribute to a successful micro-teach. For instance, if learners are expected to be able to 'state' and 'explain' concepts and principles by the end of a 20 minutes micro-teach session, this is more achievable than expecting them to 'analyse' a concept or principle. The key exception to this is where the learners already possess a sufficient understanding of the principles and concepts and are able to state and explain them. The micro-teach would then take account of the prior learning, knowledge and/or experience and move on to 'analysis'. Even then, 20 minutes might not be sufficient time to ensure all learners are able to analyse fully and check learning accordingly.[2]

Delivery considerations

The points below are relevant to planning and delivering a micro-teach or a full lesson:

- A logical structure to the session
- Appropriate pace of delivery
- Sufficient pauses to check learning

---

[1] If one considers the structure of Bloom's Taxonomy, the command verbs like 'list', 'outline', 'explain' are likely to be classed as requiring 'lower order' thinking skills, while command verbs like 'analyse', 'evaluate', 'discuss' are likely to be classed as requiring 'higher order' thinking skills. Higher order thinking skills are more demanding and complex to acquire and demonstrate than lower order thinking skills (see further: http://geoffpetty.com/wp-content/uploads/2012/12/1BloomsTaxonomycopy2)

[2] The assessment tasks are likely to be more involved and require more time.

- Commensurate level of language used
- Delivering at the right level
- Alignment to awarding organisation or course requirements
- Effective presentation:
  - PowerPoint slides (with sparing use of text, and multi-media content where appropriate)
  - Positive body language
  - Audience engagement / participation
  - Appropriate register and intonation
- Appropriate range of assessment methods used, with consistent and effective implementation of reasonable adjustments.
- Taking account of key professional standards and codes of practice
- Taking account of the Ofsted Common Inspection Framework 2015 (and the Further education and skills inspection handbook for inspections from September 2015)

Each of these is considered in detail below.

A logical structure to the session

The following should provide an initial guide and rationale for adopting a logical structure to a session:

- There should be a coherent beginning, middle and end to the session;
- Principles, concepts, theories and instructions should start from basic elements and then become increasingly complex (relative to the audience's starting point or existing knowledge and experience of these);
- Command verbs should be sequenced from those requiring lower order thinking skills (e.g. 'list', 'state', 'summarise') and then move on to those requiring higher order learning skills (e.g. 'analyse', 'evaluate', 'discuss');
- Chronological order should be maintained for certain topics (e.g. history, development of systems), unless post-modernist techniques are being deployed to make the topic more interesting, especially in literature, media and film related topics[1];

---

[1] Quentin Tarantino is a good example of an American film director that uses 'flash-backs' to explain character background and deviates from a logical chronological sequence for character and plot development, with notable success.

- Learners with dyslexia and ADHD are likely to benefit most from a logical structure to the session, as might those new to a subject or returning to education after a prolonged break from formal education and training;
- It makes it easier for a lesson observer to follow the session, especially if it is not one of their specialist subjects;
- Deviations from a logical structure might be acceptable for particular topics or for certain learners, but they normally require a great deal of experience to ensure they are executed effectively.

Possible features of a logical structure:

Beginning
- Links / brief recap of previous session key points and how they link to this session or generally to the course;
- Clear set of learning objectives for the session, outlined and explained to the learners and checked during the session and at the end;
- Outline of ground rules;
- Outline of assessment methods to be used in the session.

Middle
- Topics are effectively introduced or developed;
- There is regular checking of learning;
- A learner-centred approach is adopted;
- Where topics are to be continued in a future session, the current topic aspect is completed as far as possible in order to ensure effective progression to the next element in the future session.

End
- Check the session has achieved the lesson objectives;
- Links to the next session and outline of preparatory steps learners need to take for the next session.

Other
- Individual learner needs have been fully anticipated and met during delivery (e.g. application of planned reasonable adjustments) at effective points during the session;

- Every element of the session has a consistently logical structure, although timings might stray in exceptional circumstances where learners are providing high quality responses and their engagement is likely to exceed the planned learning for the session (this is relatively rare, hence why some deviation might be justified for the overall benefit that might accrue for learning and understanding from more time being allocated to this activity than originally planned).

Further research:

How to open and close presentations? - Presentation lesson from Mark Powell, Mark Powell, CUP (https://www.youtube.com/watch?v=Yl_FJAOcFgQ)

Appropriate pace of delivery

- The pace of delivery should be appropriate to the needs of every learner;
- Where checks on learning indicate a difficulty in understanding a principle or concept, more time should be allocated to ensuring learners understand it before moving on to more complex related principles or concepts;
- Where learners understand a principle or concept fully and more quickly than planned, the pace can be accelerated accordingly;
- Different learners tend to learn at different rates, with different levels of input and guidance. Where there is a significant divergence in the rate of learning, differentiation strategies should be employed to compensate (e.g. more support for learners falling behind, some additional challenging activities for those that are keeping-up and extension activities for those that are ahead or have prior knowledge or experience);
- During a course, the pace in individual sessions might vary significantly depending on the topics being taught, proximity to examinations and assessments, complexity of principles and concepts being taught and the overall time remaining for delivery of the programme.

Sufficient pauses to check learning

Pauses to check learning can take a number of forms. For example:

- A pause after asking a question to the entire group, awaiting voluntary responses from learners;
- A pause after asking a question to the entire group, followed by a learner being selected to answer the question;
- A pause in delivery to set quick or more formal checks on learning (e.g. question and answer, an assessment exercise or short test);
- A pause during assessments to confirm learning is taking place effectively. This also allows an opportunity to provide summative and formative feedback and clarify particular points.

Commensurate level of language used

The standard of English, number of clauses used in a sentence, length of sentences, complexity of terms used should be aligned to the level of the programme and adjusted to meet learner needs, knowledge and experience.

For example, the standard and complexity of English language used for a level 2 group of learners (equivalent to GCSE level), with an average age of 16, during delivery and assessment tasks is likely to be much lower than that used for a level 7 group of learners (equivalent to a post-graduate or Master's level), with an average age of 25. A number of awarding organisations expect the level of language used to be taken into account when setting assessments.

Consider the following example, with tasks that effectively ask the same thing, but are phrased differently and target learners at different levels.

"The principle of parliamentary supremacy in the UK is an anachronism. Discuss" (more appropriate for level 4-6 learners)

"Discuss the extent to which the UK Parliament is free to make and pass its own laws." (More appropriate for level 3 learners)

"Discuss how the EU influences legislation made and passed in the UK" (More appropriate for level 2 learners)

Implications for delivery and assessment:

- Ensure that the level and complexity of English language used during delivery and in learning and assessment materials is aligned to awarding organisation expectations and meets the needs of all learners (additional guidance might be required for those whose first language is not English);
- Provide a glossary, where needed, to define technical terms used in learning materials or to refer learners to other resources which provide such definition or further related information;
- Do not assume that where learners are not asking for clarification that they understand the terms, concepts or principles being used. Many learners might be embarrassed to raise their hand in class and say they don't understand. Therefore, regular checking of learning is important in a session;
- If you are new to teaching, then seek the advice and guidance of a seasoned practitioner or colleague on the appropriateness of your learning materials and planned delivery to ensure that you are delivering using the most appropriate language for that level and language that your learners can understand.

Delivering at the right level

"How do you know you are delivering at the right level?"

This is a question you might be asked at an inspection or review (more likely review). There are two key documents that you should be aware of. These are:

Regulatory arrangements for the Qualifications and Credit Framework (08/2008), Ofqual[1] (see in

particular Annex E: QCF level descriptors) (these cover level descriptors from entry 1 to level 8);

The framework for higher education qualifications in England, Wales and Northern Ireland (08/2008) (in particular Section 4: Qualification descriptors) (these cover level descriptors from level 4 to level 8 and apply mainly to Foundation Degrees, BTEC HNC/HND's and undergraduate and post-graduate degrees awarded by universities).

Level descriptors outline what learners should know, understand and be able to demonstrate at each level of a qualification. Level descriptors inform the design of qualifications. In an interview situation, being able to make reference to a range of relevant practitioner documents should create a good impression, so long as you have read and understood them. Knowledge of level descriptors is probably more relevant when applying to teach on higher education programmes.

Alignment to awarding organisation or course requirements

Where you have designed your own micro-teach session and it does not relate to an awarding organisation qualification, you do not need to consider alignment of what you are delivering to awarding organisation requirements.

If you are delivering a topic taken from a qualification unit, then delivery of content and use of command verbs for assessments should be aligned to qualification specifications. You should avoid delivering topics that are outside of the qualification content, unless the learning provider is seeking additionality (i.e. providing additional learning to enhance learners' progression opportunities). This is particularly relevant if you have been invited for interview and asked to prepare a micro-teach linked to the qualification specification that the learning provider delivers.

---

[1]

https://www.gov.uk/government/uploads/system/uploads /attachment_data/file/371294/2008-08-15-regulatory-arrangements-qcf-august08.pdf QCF rules themselves are currently under review and are planned to be removed: http://www.eal.org.uk/sectors/147-news/qualifications-news/1046-announcement-on-withdrawing-the-qcf-rules

Some follow-up questions might well be linked to the qualification specification (e.g. "How would you delivery the Research Methods unit?"). Each awarding organisation publishes qualification specifications and most make them available to the general public to download from the unsecured part of their website.

If you are preparing a micro-teach session with an academic topic, an awarding organisation qualification specification might provide you with more clarity about the content to be delivered, approach to assessment and command verbs to be used. Past examination papers, where available, might also provide ideas for assessment tasks / questions.

PowerPoint slides (with sparing use of text, and multi-media content embedded where appropriate)

A number of presentation approaches can be adopted with PowerPoint slides. One advisable approach is to have key points stated on slides, with each point appearing at a mouse click. This ensures learners are focused on the latest point being discussed. Where all points on the slide are displayed learners are likely to read ahead and lose focus on the current point being explored. A more advanced approach in PowerPoint is to have the latest point scroll in and the previous point dim.

Here is an example.

Slide one shows the title of the topic being addressed by the slide. On left mouse click, the first bullet point to be discussed appears and the heading dims (see below).

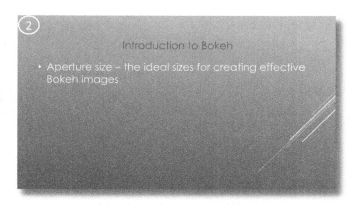

Once this topic has been discussed, the left mouse button can be clicked. This will introduce the next bullet point and the previous bullet point will dim as well. (See slide below.)

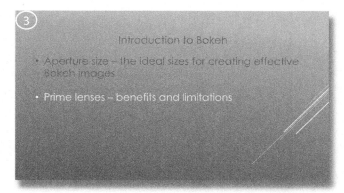

This approach ensures that learners' attention is focused on the current point being explored. The bullet points are also kept brief, with the expectation that the lecturer / presenter will expand on each bullet point, as opposed to facing towards and reading off a slide filled with text.

In MS PowerPoint, the 'animations' tab has the features required to implement the entry, exit and dimming of text (see below).

Photographic content can be included at appropriate points (see below).

Media content can be embedded in the slides at appropriate points where it adds value to the micro-teach (see example below).

Prezi software provides a truly stunning approach to delivering creative and inspiring presentations.[1] However, the learning curve is steep and it is time consuming to develop an effective presentation.[2] Is it worth investing the time and effort to design and deliver a presentation using Prezi? If it demonstrates advanced use of technology, creativity, 'stands out from the crowd' at the job interview, then the answer is a resounding 'YES'.

I recall when I designed and delivered an innovative presentation to colleagues, who were middle and senior management of a college, using bespoke photographs and advanced features of PowerPoint to make a boring topic exciting, it fully engaged the audience. I had included a photograph of one of the senior managers in the PowerPoint, with thought

bubbles introducing the presentation (with her consent of course), thereby making a personal and humorous connection with the audience.

The title was innovative, the content had various entry and exit transitions and there was a very logical structure. It had the desired impact and I overheard one of the middle managers, who was due to deliver his presentation next, say to a colleague "How do I follow that?" During the presentation, the Principal stopped me mid-delivery and said "forget about the content, how did you do that?" Prezi software, when used effectively, has a similar impact.

When I prepared that presentation, I knew that my colleagues already had an idea about the topic I was going to deliver, so the content was less important than the way it was delivered. It was also the most dry topic of our 'away day' and I needed to find innovative ways to make it engaging. Most importantly, I had a good idea what would work with the audience. The only person that was not impressed by the presentation was an IT manager, who understood the techniques used, but then you cannot impress everyone. However, he did find the content and subsequent exercises useful.

Key points to remember about PowerPoint presentations

- *Do you know the audience you are delivering to?* If so, you may have some idea what they prefer and what engages and impresses them. The presentation can be adapted accordingly;

- *Is it a competitive context, such as a job interview?* If so, you should adopt a professional approach to the presentation, i.e. using an acceptable design, applying advanced features of PowerPoint only where they enhance the professional nature of the presentation, ensuring an appropriate font type and size are used, avoid using too many colours. Slide transitions should be consistent (i.e. select one or two slide transitions). You want to make sure that the audience is focused on the content of your slides rather than special effects. The interview panel are likely to have seen and used thousands of PowerPoints and are likely to be familiar with

---

[1] https://prezi.com/

[2] See the following link for a good example of a Prezi presentation:
https://www.youtube.com/watch?v=M0k3giXi8eM

many of the advanced features of PowerPoint. I recall a lecturer who delivered a whole college presentation that 'wowed' the audience. It adopted a very clean, professional, innovative, yet simple, design. Very little text was used. The images applied complemented the story being told. She then applied for a position at another college. They could not believe that she was a recently qualified teacher and called her back for an additional interview with a more senior panel. Suffice to say she secured the position and made rapid progress;

- *Avoid using too much text or making your slides cluttered with content.* Too much text makes the audience work hard in the wrong way. Do you want your audience to focus on reading the text on the PowerPoint slides or listen to what you have to say? If you have ever watched any of the late Steve Jobs'[1] presentations, then you will have noticed that he adopts a very minimalist approach to slides;[2]

- *Consider what makes an effective presentation and apply appropriate principles to your presentation.* A good starting point to designing and delivering your PowerPoint presentation is to take on board some suggestions from a presentation expert like Garr Reynolds.[3] Another good authority is David Philips[4]

Complementary learning resources

A PowerPoint presentation can be enhanced by the use of a whiteboard and/or a flip chart and handouts. A whiteboard or flip chart can be used to capture ideas, points, answers or feedback from learners. It can also be used to draw diagrams or mind maps with input from learners. This allows for active

learner participation, and by noting their points it should increase learner motivation.

Handouts with detailed diagrams, pictures and information can be combined with PowerPoint slides. Where complex diagrams are required, these can be printed on A3 size handouts. Tables and other information which are not likely to be displayed effectively on PowerPoint slides can be printed on A4 size handouts and discussed. This adds some interaction and activity for learners, thereby potentially increasing engagement and participation. Handouts can be noted at particular points on a slide, acting as a prompt to refer to them (see example below).

Prompt for Handout 1

Positive body language

'Do'
- Face the learners;
- Maintain reasonable eye contact with as many learners as possible when delivering a presentation;
- Control physical movement, ensuring it is used for emphasis (e.g. using fingers to count points being made or to point to elements on the PowerPoint slides, etc);
- Use appropriate facial expressions when engaging with or responding to learners;
- Be responsive and sensitive to the body language of learners and how your body language responds to theirs (e.g. if a learner provides an incorrect response, shaking your head side to side to indicate 'no' is not ideal and could be demoralising. Instead a response might be to nod vertically in a brief 'yes' or acknowledgement

---

[1] Steve Jobs was the co-founder of Apple.
[2] See: https://www.youtube.com/watch?v=iJq-thyDF9Q for an analysis of Steve Jobs' presentation style.
[3] https://www.youtube.com/watch?v=vFDm1-Dvdyc
https://www.youtube.com/watch?v=DZ2vtQCESpk
(presentation to Google) and
https://www.youtube.com/watch?v=9g8T8MsFIp0
(presentation about Bamboo - It is useful to see how he makes a potentially boring plant like bamboo appear intriguing)
[4] https://www.youtube.com/watch?v=Iwpi1Lm6dFo

movement, but then state the following "I can understand why you might say that …. but …" This is more courteous and non-confrontational);

- Move around from time to time. Standing in one place can become boring;
- Presentations can be made standing up or sitting down or a combination. If you are new to presenting, delivering a presentation standing up is advisable. A lot depends on your relationship with the learners, the number of learners you are delivering to and the degree of formality for the event;
- Maintain a reasonable distance from learners (i.e. respect personal space).

'Don't'

- Have your back to learners when reading a point from the PowerPoint slide. It is better to stand at one side of the screen at a 90 degree angle so that you are able to read the point and still have the learners in your peripheral vision. It also makes it easier to turn around to face the learners;
- Have random or nervous hand movements;
- Pace or walk around too much;
- Stand motionless in one spot for a long time;
- Cross arms or legs, since this tends to be perceived as a defensive posture;
- Have excessive eye contact with any one learner;
- Roll your eyes or shrug your shoulders in response to a learner, since it can be interpreted negatively;
- Make physical contact of any kind with learners unless it is an integral and an unavoidable part of learning.

Further research:

Make Body Language Your Superpower, Stanford Graduate School of Business (https://www.youtube.com/watch?v=cFLjudWTuGQ)

Body Language Expert Mark Bowden at TEDx Toronto - The Importance Of Being Inauthentic (https://www.youtube.com/watch?v=rk_SMBIW1mg)

Mark Bowden: 10 Body Language Hacks That Instantly Boost Your State Of Mind (https://www.youtube.com/watch?v=vSuaPzc6de4)

How to kill your body language Frankenstein and inspire the villagers: Scott Rouse at TEDx Nashville (https://www.youtube.com/watch?v=Ro2dgzXKJfQ)

Audience engagement / participation

Audience or learner engagement and participation are important in all contexts. Failure to involve learners in a session can reduce the extent of learning, quality of learner experience, as well as learner morale and motivation.

Learner involvement can take the following forms:

- Questions and answers to check learning during delivery;
- Discussions relating to a topic;
- Sharing of prior learning and experience relating to the topic with peers;
- Mini planned and unplanned presentations and group written and/or verbal feedback from tasks;
- Formal and informal assessments;
- Self-assessment and peer assessment;
- Noting and displaying key points made by learners;
- Group work facilitated by the presenter.

Further research:

Think Fast, Talk Smart: Communication Techniques, Stanford Graduate School of Business (https://www.youtube.com/watch?v=Hanw168huqA)

Generating Student Participation , UCI Media Services (https://www.youtube.com/watch?v=YiuPS_p80u4)

Active Lecturing with PowerPoint, David Wicks (https://www.youtube.com/watch?v=cli2vJ116RU)

The Surprising Uses of PowerPoint to Increase Student Engagement, Klaus Woelk, Missouri University of Science and Technology (https://www.youtube.com/watch?v=Op5BdKqNbr0)

Appropriate register and intonation

When delivering your micro-teach ensure you vary the speed, volume, tone and pitch of your voice. Ensure pauses are at appropriate points and the tone matches the words used and the context. Avoid having a monotone voice. Here is an extreme example of what a monotone voice sounds like: https://www.youtube.com/watch?v=uhiCFdWeQfA (taken from the film *Ferris Bueller's Day Off*).

Contrast this with the Harvard Commencement Speech by J.K. Rowling (https://www.youtube.com/watch?v=wHGqp8lz36c).

Your content may be excellent, but if your delivery is 'flat', without sufficient intonation, you are not likely to do justice to the content being delivered.

Further research:

Speaking Tips: Is Your Speaking Voice Hurting Your Social Life?, Lauren Zapko (https://www.youtube.com/watch?v=B2Dsdw-1YU4)

Want to sound like a leader? Start by saying your name right, Laura Sicola, TEDx Penn (https://www.youtube.com/watch?v=02EJ1IdC6tE)

Appropriate range of assessment methods used, with consistent and effective implementation of reasonable adjustments

Appropriate assessment methods should be selected and used in the micro-teach and planned for a full session. The following points should be considered when selecting and using assessment methods:

- Will they generate sufficient, valid and reliable evidence to meet the assessment objectives?
- Is there sufficient time to apply the assessment methods effectively?
- Are the learners familiar with what is expected of them during assessments and the planned assessment methods in particular (e.g. it may not be appropriate to expect short presentations from learners if they have no experience of presenting or are reluctant to present)?
- Will the assessment methods ensure triangulation of evidence, confirming the authenticity and reliability of evidence produced?
- Are the assessment methods capable of supporting differentiation (e.g. exercises with differing levels of difficulty)?
- Have you used these assessment methods before; how confident are you in using them correctly in a micro-teach or answering questions about them in a job interview?
- How will you apply summative and formative feedback to the assessment methods being applied and how will you ensure learners understand that feedback?
- What will you do if the planned reasonable adjustments prove inadequate or ineffective during the micro-teach? Do you have a contingency plan / alternative reasonable adjustments?
- Avoid using too many assessment methods. Each assessment method requires a learner to demonstrate a particular skill; the more assessment methods that are used the broader the skills range required. For instance, if there is a combination of a written exercise, a practical exercise and a presentation, the skills range required for all three is relatively high, since most learners might be good at one or two of these, especially if they have limited or no experience of one or more of these assessment methods or have been out of formal education for a long time;
- Complementary assessment methods might be more appropriate, such as you observing a practical or presentation, learners completing a presentation and role play, being observed for both and giving and receiving verbal peer feedback on these. Presentations, role play and giving and receiving verbal feedback tend to require a particular skill set (i.e. kinaesthetic, visual, speaking and listening). There is limited use of writing, so this range might suit a confident learner, who enjoys socialising, likes practical tasks and is less confident in completing written exercises.
- The assessment methods should, as far as practicable, be aligned to the individual needs of learners.

Taking account of key professional standards and codes of practice

Professional Standards for Teachers and Trainers in Education and Training - England

These professional standards were published in 2014 by the Education & Training Foundation, with the purpose of supporting teachers and trainers to maintain and improve standards of teaching and learning and outcomes for learners. The standards most relevant to planning, delivery and evaluation of the micro-teach are examined below.

Standard	Possible indicators	Expected outcomes
Be creative and innovative in selecting and adapting strategies to help learners to learn	• Involving learners in the learning and assessment process (e.g. consulting learners about preferred learning styles and assessment methods and training them to interpret task, question and assessment criteria requirements); • Using new methods and technologies; • Adapting teaching, learning and assessment strategies to meet individual learning needs, including applying timely and effective reasonable adjustments.	• Learner outcomes improve; • Learners demonstrate clear understanding of task, question and assessment criteria requirements; • Positive learner feedback; • Increased learner engagement and participation when using new methods or technologies; • Improved engagement, participation, performance and positive learner feedback. • Learners with disabilities, learning difficulties or medical conditions perform well despite their disadvantage or barrier to learning, as a direct result of the reasonable adjustments applied.
Value and promote social and cultural diversity, equality of opportunity and inclusion	• Frequency of group working; • Peer assessment; • Equality and diversity is embedded in the curriculum; • Recognition of prior learning; • Learners opinions are encouraged and valued in lessons; • Assessments methods and learning materials used are sensitive to equality and diversity issues (e.g. assessment deadlines do not conflict with religious festivals).	• Regular and effective group working and peer assessments; • Learner surveys are positive about equality and diversity matters at curriculum level; • Appropriate unit exemptions; • Increased learner participation in lessons; • Reduced resubmission and retake rates, increased timely submission of work, improved performance.

Standard	Possible indicators	Expected outcomes
Apply theoretical understanding of effective practice in teaching, learning and assessment drawing on research and other evidence	• Relevant research and experience inform strategies; • Learning provider plans, policies, procedures, practices and strategies inform own strategies; • Careful attention paid to individual learner needs and strategies adapted to meet such needs.	• Improved lesson observations and learner performance; • Strategies are aligned effectively to learning provider expectations and strategies; • Improved learner experience, participation, performance and narrowing of achievement gaps across different groups of learners.
Promote the benefits of technology and support learners in its use	• Actively make and promote use of relevant technology that complements and enhances the unit or course; • Use part of a session or additional sessions to ensure learners are trained in effective use of the technology; • Technologies may be subject specific or generic (e.g. use of the Virtual Learning Environment).	• Schemes of work and lesson plans embed use of relevant technology in sessions; • Lesson observations confirm effective use of relevant technology and related learner support; • Lecturers are clear about the learning provider's policies, procedures and strategies for using relevant technology.
Enable learners to share responsibility for their own learning and assessment, setting goals that stretch and challenge	• Inclusion of self and peer assessments in sessions; • Inclusion of extension exercises / tasks in sessions aligned to individual learning needs, ability and aptitude.	• Learners internalise task requirements and marking grids by undertaking self and peer assessments; • Lesson observations confirm effective differentiated learning activities, with all learners remaining on task and working productively in the session.
Plan and deliver effective learning programmes for diverse groups or individuals in a safe and inclusive environment	• Full account is taken in sessions of health and safety and equality and diversity; • Sessions are differentiated according to individual learning needs and paced accordingly.	• Lesson plans include considerations of health and safety and equality and diversity; • Schemes of work and lesson plans have effective differentiation strategies in place. Their implementation is confirmed during lesson and peer observations.

Standard	Possible indicators	Expected outcomes
Apply appropriate and fair methods of assessment and provide constructive and timely feedback to support progression and achievement	• Assessment methods are aligned to awarding organisation requirements, expectations and guidance; • Assessment methods take account of learner needs and training is provided to learners to adjust to new assessment methods before formal / summative assessment; • Summative and formative feedback are provided at appropriate intervals in order to maximise learner performance.	• Awarding organisation reports from External Examiners, Standards Verifiers are positive about assessment methods used; • Reasonable adjustments have been made and positively impacted on learners receiving them. Learners are confident undertaking assessments and resubmission / retake rates have reduced; • Learner performance has improved. Learner comments on feedback is positive. All feedback is detailed and constructive. This is confirmed during lesson observations, sampling, internal verification, quality assurance activities.
Reflect on what works best in your teaching and learning to meet the diverse needs of learners	• Lecturers reflect on their teaching, learning and assessment practice after each session and identify the most suitable strategies that meet the needs of their learners in each group.	• There is evidence of adjustments being made to teaching, learning and assessment strategies for each group in order to meet their particular learning needs. This is evidenced by amended schemes of work and lesson plans for one or more groups of learners. • Lesson observations confirm increased learner engagement and participation in sessions; • Learner performance improves; • Learner feedback is positive.
Evaluate and challenge your practice, values and beliefs	• Lecturers undertake self-evaluation of their practice and actively consider improvements and enhancements to their practice on a continual basis.	• There is a reflective log; • Action and development plans focus on improvement and development and are followed in a timely manner; • CPD log, with evidence of training for new or different teaching, learning and assessment strategies.

Special educational needs and disability (SEND) code of practice: 0 to 25 years[1]

The Special educational needs and disability (SEND) code of practice was introduced in January 2015. It applies to individuals up to the age of 25 and extends to the further education sector. This includes further education (FE) colleges, sixth form colleges, 16-19 academies and some independent specialist colleges. FE colleges, sixth form colleges, 16-19 academies and independent specialist colleges approved under section 41 of the Children and Families Act 2014 have the following specific statutory duties:

- The duty to co-operate with the local authority on arrangements for children and young people[2] with special educational needs (SEN)[3];

- The duty to admit a young person if the institution is named in an Educational Health and Care (EHC) plan;

- The duty to have regard to the SEND code of practice;

- The duty to use their best endeavours to secure the special educational provision that the young person needs.

The special educational support that needs to be provided includes the following (this is not an exhaustive list):

- assistive technology

- personal care (or access to it)

- specialist tuition

- note takers

- interpreters

- one-to-one and small group learning support

- independent living training

- accessible information, such as symbol based materials

- access to therapies (e.g. speech and language therapy)

Taking account of the Ofsted Common Inspection Framework 2015 (and the Further education and skills inspection handbook for inspections from September 2015)

Learning providers that are publicly funded up to level 3 are likely to be inspected by Ofsted. The two most important outcomes for a learning provider are 'Outstanding' (Grade 1) and 'Good' (Grade 2). Anything lower than these two grades can result in follow-up inspections or re-inspections.

Ofsted grades a learning provider as follows:

'Outstanding' - Grade 1

'Good' - Grade 2

'Requires improvement' - Grade 3

'Inadequate' - Grade 4

Learning providers expect their lecturing and training staff to be at least 'Good' or Grade 2 during lesson observations and generally. Anything less can trigger support and follow-up lesson observations and possibly capability proceedings.

It is therefore important that lecturers, trainers and assessors intending to work on a publicly funded programme inspected by Ofsted are familiar with the relevant aspects of the Ofsted common inspection framework and related inspection handbook and ensure that these inform the planning, development and review of their sessions. These are considered in outline in the next few pages.

---

[1] A copy of the code can be found at:
https://www.gov.uk/government/uploads/system/uploads/attachment_data/file/398815/SEND_Code_of_Practice_January_2015.pdf

[2] Young people are individuals aged between 16 to 25.

[3] A young person has SEN if they have a learning difficulty or disability which requires a special educational provision to be made for them. Special educational provision is support which is additional or different to support usually available to young people of the same age in mainstream colleges. Colleges should offer an inclusive approach to learning and teaching, with high quality teaching which is differentiated for individuals. This approach should be embedded in their provision in all subject areas, at all levels and support the teaching of all learners, including those with SEN (p. 113 SEND code of practice).

Grade descriptor heading	Outstanding (Grade 1) (selected grade descriptors)	Good (Grade 2) (selected grade descriptors)	Implications for micro-teach, lesson planning and delivery and a possible response
Quality of teaching, learning and assessment	Learners are curious, interested and keen to learn. They seek out and use new information to develop, consolidate and deepen their knowledge, understanding and skills. They thrive in learning sessions and, where appropriate, use their experiences in the workplace to further develop their knowledge, skills and understanding.	Most learners enjoy their learning across the provision. Teaching challenges them and enables them to develop, consolidate and deepen their knowledge, understanding and skills well.	• Provide and promote access to and use of a range of additional learning resources; • Fully involve and engage all learners in sessions; • Provide challenging tasks wherever possible.
	Learners are eager to know how they can improve their work and develop their knowledge, understanding and skills. They capitalise on opportunities to use feedback to improve. Staff check learners' understanding systematically and effectively, offering clearly directed and timely support that has a notable impact on improving learning.	Most learners want to know how to improve their learning and act on feedback to help them to improve. Staff listen to, carefully observe and skilfully question learners during learning sessions. They reshape tasks and explanations and provide feedback to tackle misconceptions and build on learners' strengths. This has a positive impact on learning.	• Provide timely, frequent, constructive and detailed summative and formative feedback in different forms (e.g. written, verbal, electronic), with SMART action plans; • Make effective use of question and answer techniques to check learning during sessions.
	Staff plan learning sessions and assessments very effectively so that all learners undertake demanding work that helps them to realise their potential. Staff identify and support any learner who is falling behind and enable almost all to catch up.	Staff assess learners' knowledge and understanding frequently to ensure that they are making at least the expected progress throughout their time with the provider, including the time spent at work or on work experience. Staff use this information well to plan activities in which learners undertake demanding work that helps them to make strong progress. They identify and support effectively those learners who start to fall behind.	• Prompt action is taken to support learners that might be falling behind in a session; • Learning resources are differentiated well; • Sessions include a range of assessment activities to check learning.

Grade descriptor heading	Outstanding (Grade 1) (selected grade descriptors)	Good (Grade 2) (selected grade descriptors)	Implications for micro-teach, lesson planning and delivery and a possible response
	Staff set work that consolidates learning, deepens understanding and develops skills, and prepares learners very well for their next steps.	Staff set work that builds on previous learning, extends learners' knowledge and understanding and develops their skills to ensure that they are prepared for their future.	• Progressively challenging tasks are set in sessions and differentiated effectively, with robust support mechanisms and extension activities in place; • Tasks and assessments are appropriately sequenced, moving from pass to higher grades at a pace learners can manage.
	Staff are quick to challenge stereotypes and the use of derogatory language, including at work. Resources and teaching strategies reflect and value the diversity of learners' experiences and provide learners with a comprehensive understanding of people and communities beyond their immediate experience.	Staff promote equality of opportunity and diversity in teaching and learning.	• A zero-tolerance approach is adopted to discrimination, anti-social behaviour and derogatory remarks in class; • Learning resources include a diverse range of scenarios, case studies or examples, taking account of other socio-economic and racial communities and going beyond local and national boundaries / contexts; • Equality and diversity are embedded into the curriculum, although not fully.
Outcomes for learners	Learners, and groups of learners, are typically able to articulate their knowledge and understanding clearly and demonstrate the skills they have acquired convincingly. The standard of learners' work is high and, where appropriate, meets industry standards very well.	The standard of learners' work meets or exceeds that expected for the level of their course and, where appropriate, the relevant industry. Learners from across different groups can explain how they have developed and what they have learnt.	• The quality of learners' assessment responses / outcomes in sessions are high relative to their starting points (i.e. their prior learning, qualifications and experience) and they can demonstrate what they have learnt effectively.

Grade descriptor heading	Outstanding (Grade 1) (selected grade descriptors)	Good (Grade 2) (selected grade descriptors)	Implications for micro-teach, lesson planning and delivery and a possible response
The effectiveness of the 16 to 19 study programmes	Teaching, learning and assessment support and challenge learners to make substantial and sustained progress in all aspects of their study programme. Teaching enables learners who fall behind to catch up swiftly and the most able to excel.	Teaching, learning and assessment support and challenge learners so that they make strong progress across all aspects of their study programmes. Learners who fall behind are helped to catch up and the most able are stretched.	• Teaching, learning and assessment are effective in meeting all learners' needs (e.g. application of reasonable adjustments, differentiation strategies) and as a result they make significant and continued progress during sessions; • Lecturers identify learners falling behind in sessions and actively support them to catch-up quickly.
	Learners are safe and feel safe. They are thoughtful, caring and respectful citizens. They take responsibility for keeping themselves safe and healthy and contribute to wider society and life in Britain.	Learners are safe and feel safe. They behave well, respect others and understand how to keep themselves safe and healthy and to contribute to wider society and life in Britain.	• Health and safety is planned, implemented and shared effectively with learners, who take responsibility for remaining safe while in the classroom and during external visits; • Learners are considerate and respectful to others (e.g. peer tutoring, peer assessment); • Learners do not discriminate and are sensitive to other learners' feelings.
The effectiveness of adult learning programmes	Teaching, learning and assessment support and challenge learners to make sustained and substantial progress in all aspects of their learning programmes. Teaching enables learners that fall behind to catch up swiftly and the most able to excel. Especially where learners are not working towards a qualification, they receive accurate and reliable records of their achievements and progress towards their individual learning goals.	Teaching, learning and assessment support and challenge learners so that they make progress across all aspects of their learning programmes. Learners who fall behind are helped to catch up and the most able are challenged to achieve particularly well. Especially where learners are not working towards a qualification, they receive useful records of their achievements and progress towards their individual learning goals.	• Teaching, learning and assessment are effective in meeting all learners' needs (e.g. application of reasonable adjustments, differentiation strategies) and as a result they make significant and continued progress; • Lecturers identify learners falling behind in sessions and actively support them to catch-up quickly; • Regular and detailed written summative feedback confirms learner progress on courses that do not lead to a formal qualification.

Grade descriptor heading	Outstanding (Grade 1) (selected grade descriptors)	Good (Grade 2) (selected grade descriptors)	Implications for micro-teach, lesson planning and delivery and a possible response
	Learners are safe and feel safe, including at work and in community settings. They are thoughtful, caring and respectful members of their community or workplace. They take responsibility for keeping themselves safe and healthy and contribute to wider society and life in Britain.	Learners are safe and feel safe, including at work and in community settings. They behave well, respect others and understand how to keep themselves safe and healthy and to contribute to wider society and life in Britain.	• Health and safety is planned, implemented and practices shared effectively with learners, who take responsibility for remaining safe while in the classroom and during external visits; • Learners are considerate and respectful to others (e.g. peer tutoring, peer assessment); • Learners do not discriminate and are sensitive to other learners' feelings.
The effectiveness of apprenticeship programmes	On- and off-the-job training is particularly well planned in consultation with employers so that they are very well-coordinated with apprentices' development at work. Training and assessment support and challenge apprentices to make sustained and substantial progress in all aspects of their programme and to develop excellent skills and knowledge to high industry standards. Training enables apprentices who fall behind to catch up swiftly and the most able to progress quickly to more complex and advanced tasks.	On- and off-the-job training is planned well in consultation with employers so that they fit in well with apprentices' development at work. Training and assessment support and challenge apprentices to make sustained and substantial progress in all aspects of their programme and to develop skills and knowledge to high industry standards.	• Session content, delivery and assessments align effectively with awarding organisation, employer and industry requirements and expectations; • Teaching, learning and assessment complement learners' development at work; • Training is differentiated effectively to provide support for those falling behind and extension / challenging activities to promote rapid progress of the most able learners; • Sessions focus on developing learners to meet the knowledge and skills aligned to high industry standards.

Grade descriptor heading	Outstanding (Grade 1) (selected grade descriptors)	Good (Grade 2) (selected grade descriptors)	Implications for micro-teach, lesson planning and delivery and a possible response
The effectiveness of traineeships	Teaching, learning and assessment, including on work experience, support and challenge learners to make sustained and substantial progress in all aspects of their traineeship. Teaching enables learners who fall behind to catch up swiftly and the most able to excel and progress to an apprenticeship.	Teaching, learning and assessment support and challenge learners so that they make the expected progress across all aspects of their traineeships. Learners who fall behind are helped to catch up and the most able are supported to achieve more quickly.	• Teaching, learning and assessment are differentiated effectively to provide support for those falling behind and extension / challenging activities to promote rapid progress of the most able learners.
	Learners are safe and feel safe, including at work. They are thoughtful, caring and respectful members of their course and on work experience. They take responsibility for keeping themselves safe and healthy, including at work, and contribute to wider society and life in Britain.	Learners are safe and feel safe. They behave well, respect others and understand how to keep themselves safe and healthy, including at work, and to contribute to wider society and life in Britain.	• Health and safety is planned, implemented and shared effectively with learners, who take responsibility for remaining safe while in the classroom, workplace and during external visits; • Learners are considerate and respectful to others (e.g. peer tutoring, peer assessment). • Learners do not discriminate and are sensitive to other learners' feelings.
The effectiveness of provision for learners with high needs	Teachers and support staff use previous assessments very effectively to support and challenge learners so that they make excellent progress across all aspects of their programmes compared with their starting points and personal circumstances. Staff are especially skilled at assessing learners' progress, adapting activities to support learners whose development is slow and providing more challenging activities for the more able learners.	Teachers and support staff use previous assessments well to support and challenge learners so that they progress well across all aspects of their programmes. Staff are skilled at assessing learners' progress, adapting activities to support learners whose development is slow and providing more challenging activities for the more able learners.	• Taking accurate account of learners' starting points (i.e. prior learning, qualifications and experience), teaching, learning and assessments seeks to maximise the performance and progress learners make during sessions and on the programme; • There is effective differentiation, with support for those who need it and extension activities for more able learners.

53

Grade descriptor heading	Outstanding (Grade 1) (selected grade descriptors)	Good (Grade 2) (selected grade descriptors)	Implications for micro-teach, lesson planning and delivery and a possible response
	Learners are safe and feel safe. They are thoughtful, caring and respectful citizens. Where appropriate, they take responsibility for keeping themselves safe and healthy and contribute to wider society and life in Britain.	Learners are safe and feel safe. They behave well, respect others and understand, where appropriate, how to keep themselves safe and healthy and to contribute to wider society and life in Britain.	• Health and safety is planned, implemented and shared effectively with learners, who take responsibility for remaining safe while in the classroom and during external visits; • Learners are considerate and respectful to others (e.g. peer tutoring, peer assessment); • Learners do not discriminate and are sensitive to other learners' feelings.
The effectiveness of full-time provision for 14- to 16-year-olds	Teaching, learning and assessment support and challenge learners to make sustained and substantial progress in all aspects of their learning programme. Teaching enables learners that fall behind to catch up swiftly and the most able to excel.	Teaching, learning and assessment support and challenge learners so that they make at least the expected progress across all aspects of their learning programmes. Learners who fall behind are helped to catch up and the most able are stretched.	• Teaching, learning and assessment are differentiated effectively to provide support for those falling behind and extension / challenging activities to promote rapid progress of the most able learners.
	Learners are safe and feel safe, including at off-site premises. They are thoughtful, caring and respectful citizens. They take responsibility for keeping themselves safe and healthy and contribute to wider society and life in Britain.	Learners are safe and feel safe. They behave well, respect others and understand how to keep themselves safe and healthy and how to contribute to wider society and life in Britain.	• Health and safety is planned, implemented and shared effectively with learners, who take responsibility for remaining safe while in the classroom and during external visits; • Learners are considerate and respectful to others (e.g. peer tutoring, peer assessment); • Learners do not discriminate and are sensitive to other learners' feelings.

A copy of the Ofsted Common Inspection Framework 2015 can be downloaded from: https://www.gov.uk/government/publications/common-inspection-framework-education-skills-and-early-years-from-september-2015 and a copy of the Ofsted Further Education and Skills Inspection Handbook 2015 can be downloaded from: https://www.gov.uk/government/publications/further-education-and-skills-inspection-handbook-from-september-2015

Presentation slides for the example micro-teach and a supporting rationale

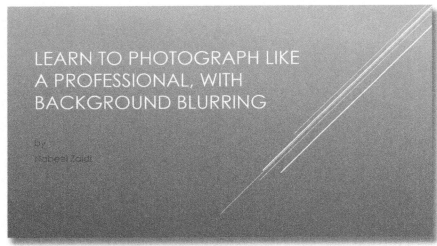

A basic PowerPoint design has been selected, since the primary focus should remain on the presenter and the demonstrations being undertaken. For this micro-teach, the PowerPoint should be viewed merely as a tool to assist in delivering information. The background is also relatively dark for this purpose, since individuals naturally focus on bright colours, which is not useful when demonstrating how to use photographic techniques while standing alongside the PowerPoint. There are situations where a bright and attractive PowerPoint presentation should be prepared. One such example is online content, where the learner is engaging directly with the PowerPoint slides and there is no presenter in the vicinity.

The session objectives are differentiated according to prior learning, experience and ability. They are aligned to the micro-teach lesson plan. The statement and sharing of session objectives are important for providing a structure to the session, ensuring clear communication to learners of what is expected of them during and by the end of the session. It also sets out the minimum expectations (i.e. "All learners will be able to …") and aspirational and/or differentiated expectations (i.e. "Some learners will be able to …"). There is nothing precluding learners without prior DSLR camera experience from attempting the more challenging tasks. For an interview situation, the above slide preempts a possible question of strategies to plan and deliver differentiated learning and ensure 'academic stretch'. As far as the course is concerned, it should demonstrate effective planning to meet individual learner needs.

Introduction to Bokeh

- Aperture size – the ideal sizes for creating effective Bokeh images
- Prime lenses – benefits and limitations
- Depth of field – the basics

The text here is kept to a minimum. Each line is introduced individually and is followed by a verbal explanation by the presenter and a physical demonstration using the DSLR camera, a 50 mm lens and related props. Subsequent slides provide further details and related photographs and video content.

Example 1: Bokeh effect using f 2.8

Post-photograph processing:

- a range of Adobe Photoshop techniques applied to the face
- overall image sharpened in Adobe Photoshop

Example 2: Bokeh effect using f 1.8

Post-photograph processing:

- overall image sharpened in Adobe Photoshop

Handout 1

The photographs use different f-stops, which directly impact on the sharpness of the image in the foreground and the level of blurring in the background. The minimum expected of learners is to photograph using f-stop 1.8 (see Example 2 in the above slide), while learners with experience of DSLR cameras should be photographing at various f-stops, including f 1.8 and f 2.8 (see Example 1 in the above slide). Delivery is the same to all learners, but what they are expected to be able to demonstrate during and by the end of the session are different. Handout 1, which is noted at the bottom of the slide, provides more detailed information that is handed out once the slide has been delivered. Some time is then set aside to discuss the handout. This varies the learning activity and avoids excessive content in the slides.

A screenshot of the You Tube video is included in the slide and hyper-linked to the same You Tube video. An extract is to be displayed and the start and end times of that extract are noted by the presenter so that only that extract is presented.

Depending on the nature of the You Tube licence, an alternative to hyper-linking to the You Tube video is to download, edit and embed the edited video in the slides. There is no title on the slide itself, since the screenshot of the video displays the necessary title. Consequently, this results in a simple and clean slide.

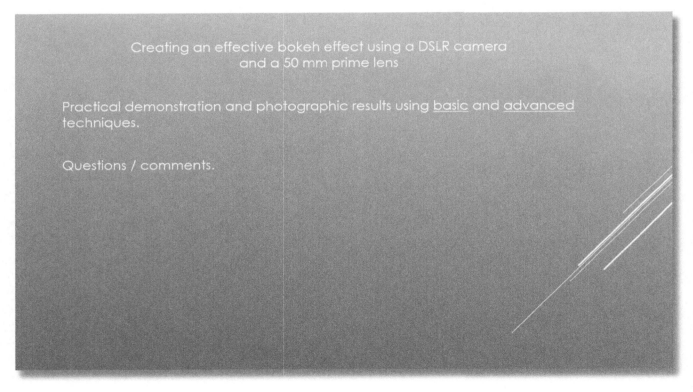

This slide states the session objective being covered and outlines the demonstration to be delivered, following which the next line is displayed in order to prompt questions and comments.

This video screenshot is of the selective focusing technique being used. The title at the top of the slide is aligned to one of the session objectives, which re-enforces the structure of the session and is a useful guide for anyone undertaking an observation of the micro-teach. They can check the extent to which the delivery is aligned to the micro-teach plan. This approach also ensures that you do not miss anything from the planned delivery.

As with some of the earlier slides, the title of the slide is aligned to one of the session objectives. The practical demonstration will include live photographs taken and these will be displayed on the data projector. Subsequent questions and comments provide an opportunity to check learning and provide clarification and guidance. The slide is minimalist, since the focus is on practical demonstration and questions.

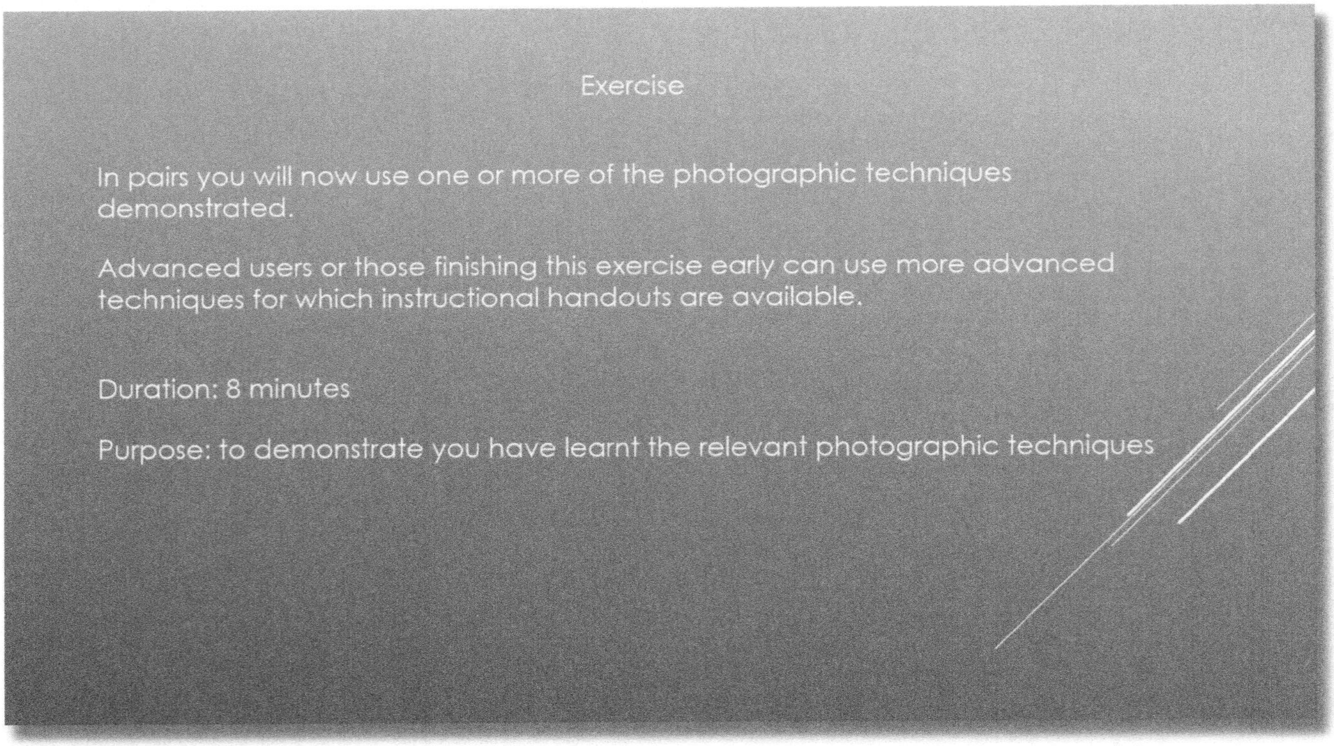

Exercise

In pairs you will now use one or more of the photographic techniques demonstrated.

Advanced users or those finishing this exercise early can use more advanced techniques for which instructional handouts are available.

Duration: 8 minutes

Purpose: to demonstrate you have learnt the relevant photographic techniques

The above slide ensures that learners are clear about the parameters, duration and purpose of the exercise.

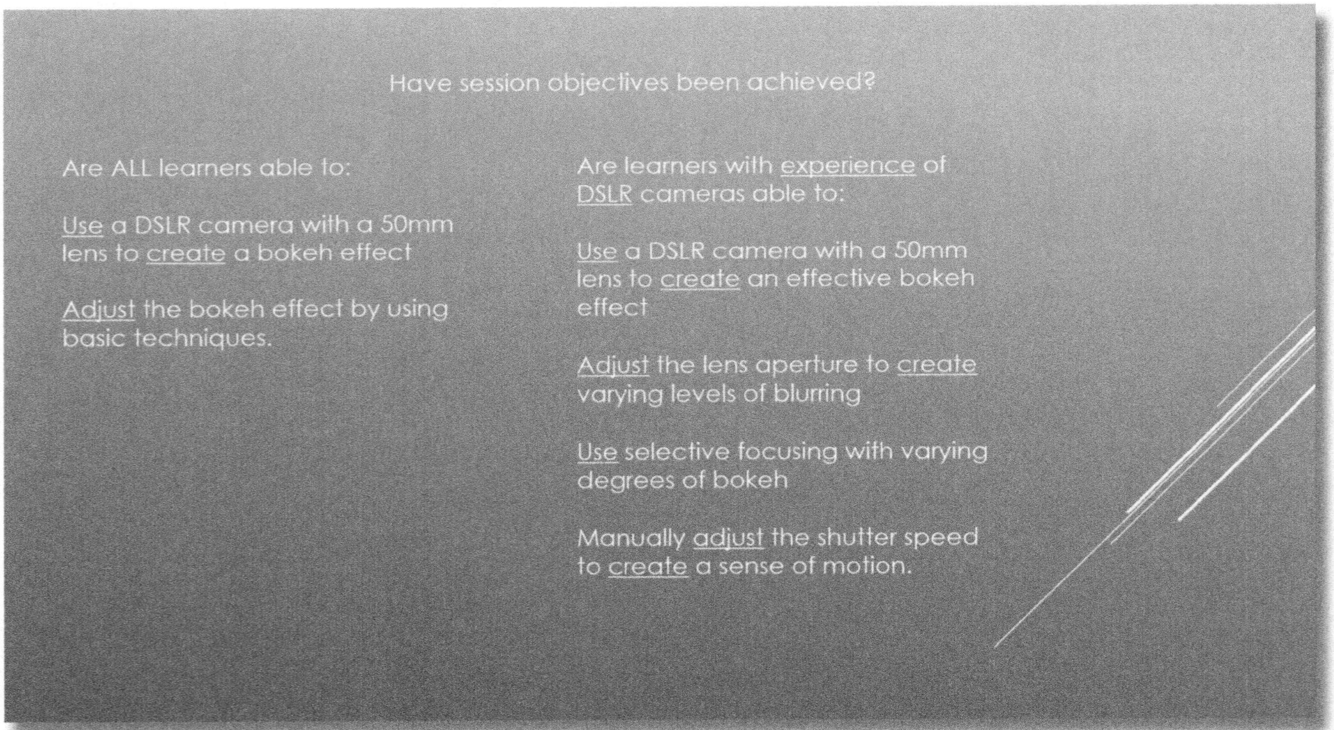

Have session objectives been achieved?

Are ALL learners able to:

Use a DSLR camera with a 50mm lens to create a bokeh effect

Adjust the bokeh effect by using basic techniques.

Are learners with experience of DSLR cameras able to:

Use a DSLR camera with a 50mm lens to create an effective bokeh effect

Adjust the lens aperture to create varying levels of blurring

Use selective focusing with varying degrees of bokeh

Manually adjust the shutter speed to create a sense of motion.

The above slide content checks the extent to which the session objectives have been achieved. This actively involves learners and promotes self-assessment / reflection. It also involves them in the assessment process and identifies possible gaps in learning that might need to be covered in the subsequent or additional session.

This slide signals the end of the presentation. A simple "Thank You" should be sufficient. You could also include "Questions and Comments" here if you wish.

Peer and tutor feedback

At the end of your micro-teach, your peers and tutor are likely to provide you with feedback (this might vary, depending on the learning provider you are completing the course at). This feedback forms an integral part of the evaluation of your micro-teach and informs your development plan. Ideally, this feedback should be video and/or audio recorded and replayed when completing your micro-teach evaluation and development plan. Your course tutor might provide written feedback in addition to or in place of verbal feedback.

Job interview initial considerations

You are not likely to receive any immediate feedback on your micro-teach during your interview. There might be verbal feedback during the day (especially if you were unsuccessful) or on formal request following an unsuccessful interview. It really depends on the policies, procedures and practices of the learning provider concerned.

You could be asked evaluative and reflective questions about your micro-teach and the rationale for the approach to planning and delivering it. It is therefore important that you adopt an evaluative and reflective approach when researching and planning your micro-teach.

You might want to consider learning provider specific information, in particular published accreditation,

inspection or review reports and any follow-up or annual monitoring visits. This could provide an initial guideline as to where they were, where they are now or likely to be in the near future and what they might be expecting from a new lecturer or trainer. For example, if you are applying to a learning provider that has recently received a Grade 1 / 'Outstanding' in an Ofsted inspection report, their expectations from the micro-teach might be quite different from a learning provider that has recently received a Grade 3 / 'Requires improvement" in their Ofsted inspection report. Do not under-estimate the importance of undertaking background research on the learning provider and the department area you are applying to.

For instance, while the learning provider might have achieved a Grade 2 / 'Good' overall in a recent Ofsted inspection report, the individual subject area might have achieved a Grade 4 / 'Inadequate'. The expectations of that department might be very specific, more so than the overall organisation. If the learning provider is agreeable, you might want to request a copy of the strategic plan and quality improvement plans. This should provide you with some idea as to their strategic and operational priorities. If it is a vocational programme area there might be standards verifier, external verifier or external examiner reports that they might be willing to provide you.

Even if you have prepared and delivered an effective micro-teach, the follow-up questions could create difficulties, especially if there are better prepared candidates or internal candidates, who are likely to have access to a lot of information and be familiar with the organisational culture, policies, procedures and practices.

Detailed examination of the learning provider website should provide some of the information you require. Accreditation, inspection and review related reports should be publicly available. If it is a private provider not in receipt of public funding, it might have received accreditation by BAC[1] or been inspected by ISI[2] or reviewed by QAA[3]. If it is in receipt of public funding, it is likely to have been inspected by Ofsted.[4] Further Education colleges with further education and higher education provision are likely to be inspected by Ofsted for entry 1 to level 3 programmes and reviewed by QAA for Level 4 to 8 programmes. If your role involves delivery across levels 3-7, you will need to be familiar with the Ofsted inspection and QAA review reports. For higher education provision, you should familiarise yourself with the UK Quality Code for Higher Education, in particular Chapters B3, B4, B6 and B8[5] and the QAA Higher Education Review handbook.[6] For providers subject to ISI inspection, you might benefit from familiarising yourself with the ISI PFE handbook[7], in particular the section on "The Quality of the Curriculum, Teaching and Learners' Achievements".

You should seek to internalise the relevant parts of the above documents that have direct implications for your role as a lecturer or trainer. Reading and familiarising yourself with awarding organisation qualification specifications and quality assurance requirements as they relate to you should also prove useful. These can often be downloaded from the awarding organisation websites. You will, however, need to confirm the awarding organisations for your programmes. If it is a validated programme delivered in partnership with a university, you may need to

request the programme specification from the learning provider directly. A programme specification should provide detailed information about the programmes being delivered.

Micro-teach checklist (course related)

At this point it might prove useful to have a checklist for researching, preparing and delivering your micro-teach on the Award in Education and Training.

Research

- Are there appropriate and sufficient resources available (are these financially and logistically viable and fit for purpose)?

- Are you clear about the existing knowledge and experience of your audience for the proposed topic(s)?

- Is it a topic that the audience are interested in receiving? and have you consulted them?

- Can the topic be delivered in the time? What is the level of complexity of the topic and will it result in the desired level of learning in the timeframe?

- Do you possess sufficient knowledge, experience and confidence to deliver the topic?

- Is your topic too similar to a colleague's topic. If so, have you considered some variation to ensure new learning takes place during your session (assuming that your micro-teach is after theirs)?

Preparatory steps

- Have you selected an appropriate title for your micro-teach - one that the audience will understand?

- Have you identified and critically reviewed the resources selected, and do you have a clear rationale for the use of these resources?

- Are the learning resources sufficiently differentiated in order to meet the needs of all learners / participants?

[1] http://www.the-bac.org/accredited-providers/directory/
[2] http://www.educationaloversight.co.uk/reports/
[3] http://www.qaa.ac.uk/reviews-and-reports
[4] http://reports.ofsted.gov.uk/
[5] http://www.qaa.ac.uk/assuring-standards-and-quality/the-quality-code/quality-code-part-b
[6] http://www.qaa.ac.uk/en/Publications/Documents/HER-AP-handbook-15.pdf (for alternative providers); http://www.qaa.ac.uk/en/Publications/Documents/HER-handbook-14.pdf (for HEFCE funded providers 2014-15); http://www.qaa.ac.uk/publications
[7] http://www.educationaloversight.co.uk/faqs/

- Have you clearly identified the expected outcome for each group of learners (i.e. by ability, prior knowledge, learning and experience)?

- Are there any anticipated reasonable adjustments. If so, identify the exact nature of the reasonable adjustments and then review the suitability of the differentiated resources in light of such reasonable adjustments.

Micro-teach lesson plan

Have the following been considered and appropriately noted in the lesson plan:

- Aims of the session

- Differentiated session objectives

- Assessment strategies that are clearly aligned to the relevant session objectives, with triangulation to ensure authenticity and reliability of the evidence generated

- Appropriate and sufficiently challenging command verbs used for assessment objectives

- Health and safety

- Equality and diversity

- Details of teaching, learning and assessment activities and resources

- A logical structure to the session, with appropriate timings and a systematic approach to topic development

- Differentiation strategies

Evaluation

Have you scheduled time shortly after your micro-teach to undertake evaluation of it?

Micro-teach checklist (job interview related)

The checklist for the interview related micro-teach has some differences, since it will be delivered in a very competitive context, sometimes with experienced candidates and a panel that is viewing the research, planning and delivery aligned to the learning provider's particular context.

Research

Learning provider related research

Online research

Learning provider website:

- Courses offered in your subject area / related to your interview

- Organisational structure

- Recent changes, improvements, enhancements, awards relevant to the department that is calling you for interview

- Strategic plan and quality improvement plan (if published)

- Policies, procedures, strategies relating to teaching, learning, assessment, quality assurance, differentiation and equality and diversity (if published)

- Staffing profiles of those people interviewing you (if disclosed and published)

- Learner performance data and any accreditation, awarding organisation or inspection and review reports published on the website.

Other websites:

- Ofsted (if Ofsted inspected)

- QAA (if reviewed by QAA)

- BAC (if accredited by BAC)

- ISI (if inspected by ISI)

- Local and national news articles / reports on the learning provider that might be relevant to your area (e.g. proposed expansion / diversification and how it could affect the lecturing role)

Direct document requests to the Human Resources Manager at the learning provider or other main contact managing the recruitment process. Documents requested could include the following:

- Strategic Plan (and related updates)

- Quality Improvement Plan

- Latest Department Self Assessment Report

- Teaching, learning and assessment strategies and/or policies

- Learner performance data for the programme area you are being interviewed for.

The above documents and information should prove useful in preparing your micro-teach, related resources and answering questions on teaching, learning and assessment.

However, there is no guarantee that the learning provider will supply all or any of the above requested documents.

Micro-teach related research

- Are there appropriate and sufficient resources available at the learning provider (e.g. software and hardware, such as PowerPoint, data projector, computer)?

- Are you clear about who you are expected to deliver to and the course that you are being interviewed to deliver on?

  - If you are delivering to learning provider staff and/or the interview panel, they might ask you to assume they are students (sometimes with details of the course and unit they are studying)

  - If you are delivering to students (normally a relatively small group), you might want to consider making the scenarios, examples used and IT elements more fun and engaging

  - If you are given a topic to deliver, with details of the awarding organisation course and unit it is taken from, then you should download the qualification specification and unit

specification from the awarding organisation website. With some courses, the unit specification provides suggested delivery and assessment strategies. Aligning your delivery accordingly should be viewed positively (or might be the minimum expected if the candidate quality attending for interview is good)

  - Actively seek up-to-date examples related to your topic from the internet and attempt to be innovative in your approach. Remember, if there are several candidates, you need to ensure your micro-teach content and examples are memorable, engaging and have the desired impact. The staff or interview panel you will be delivering to are likely to be seasoned professionals who have seen or observed and graded lessons, been trained in and/or experimented with a wide range of content, examples and learning resources

- Can the selected topic be delivered effectively in the timeframe allocated by the learning provider? Are there likely to be opportunities to check learning and how will you adapt these to the time available and the intended audience?

- Do you possess sufficient knowledge and/or experience to deliver the topic? If not, you may need to undertake some research and seek advice from an experienced lecturer or trainer who has delivered the topic

- Have you been given a task, title or topic or are you free to select your own? If you have been provided with a task, do not presume that it has been professionally drafted (it can sometimes be vague or not well constructed). If in doubt, you might want to seek clarification from the human resources department, who tend to lead on managing the communication with interviewees

- If you are selecting your own topic, consider something that is cutting-edge or of recent interest. For example, if you decide to select a business topic, such as 'marketing mix', you might decide to apply it to online businesses rather than conventional high street retailers, in part because of the growing popularity of e-tailers. If you select a topic relating to the legal profession, you might want to include not just solicitors, barristers, legal executives / para-legals, but also trademark attorneys. This is mainly because not many people are aware of the expertise and professional status of trademark attorneys in the UK, including, if you have time, to show how to search on the government database for registered trademarks. This is likely to be different from the normal delivery of the topic and provide opportunities for you to stand out from other candidates, while not deviating from the core content of the topic. For the audience it should be something very practical. If you have been set a management related topic such as 'talent management', then you could consider this in the context of new technologies, where the real difficulty lies in being able to identify the skills range needed from a new project manager to project manage an as yet undeveloped technology. This approach secured one of my mentee's a lecturing position at a global education provider. The panel were impressed by the innovative approach to the topic, which was not present in the other candidates' micro-teach.

Micro-teach lesson plan

Have the following been considered and appropriately noted in the lesson plan:

- Aims of the session

- Differentiated session objectives

- Assessment strategies that are clearly aligned to the relevant session objectives, with triangulation to ensure authenticity and reliability of the evidence generated

- Appropriate and sufficiently challenging command verbs used for assessment objectives

- Health and safety

- Equality and diversity

- Details of teaching, learning and assessment activities and resources

- A logical structure to the session, with appropriate timings and a systematic approach to topic development

- Differentiation strategies

Lesson plan

It is advisable to have a micro-teach specific lesson plan and a full lesson plan, which incorporates the micro-teach lesson plan. If you are then asked about follow-up activities, assessments, delivery of a full session, you have a frame of reference that is already pre-planned and available for ease of reference. A full lesson plan should include all the micro-teach elements above as well as the following:

- Links to the previous session and some recap

- Links to the next session

- More sustained assessment strategies

- Some higher order thinking skills reflected in challenging command verbs, such as 'analyse', 'evaluate', 'discuss'.

Evaluation

The evaluation section might be blank or you could include sample text and note it as such. Learning providers are under on-going pressure to demonstrate work towards continuous improvement. 'Evaluation' can inform this process at course level.

Practice (course related)

The importance of practicing your micro-teach should not be under-estimated. The following staged process might assist:

Stage 1

Deliver the micro-teach by yourself and work through any assessments by yourself. This will provide you with confirmation of the actual time it takes to deliver the micro-teach, which might be very different from your original planning and time estimates. Ask someone to video your micro-teach or video yourself if you have the necessary equipment. Play back the video and evaluate and reflect on your delivery. What you might well discover is that there is a gap between how you thought you delivered and what the video shows you.[1]

Stage 2

Deliver the micro-teach to friends or colleagues, ask them to complete the assessments and request constructively critical feedback. In addition, video the session if possible and play back to evaluate and review. It is not advisable to deliver the micro-teach practice session to your peers / target audience, since it will be difficult to demonstrate new learning has taken place and it is less likely to be of value to you in informing your preparation for an interview related micro-teach.

Stage 3

Make final changes or tweaks to your original micro-teach lesson plan, learning resources and assessments in light of the practice delivery.

Practice (job interview related)

The process is very similar to the above, except that your audience members should be 'critical friends' (e.g. qualified lecturers or trainers) and you might want to go through the process twice until perfected (in your mind at least). Expect one week's notice or slightly less for an interview with a micro-teach, so you need to set aside sufficient time to prepare.

Evaluation and improvement and development

You are expected to evaluate your micro-teach and use the outcome of the evaluation to inform future improvement and development.

The sources of information available to you for evaluation include the following:

- A reflection of what you considered went well and what could be improved during your delivery

- The completed self-evaluation of the lesson plan

- Feedback from your peers that observed and participated in the micro-teach

- Feedback from your course tutor that observed your micro-teach

- Your micro-teach lesson plan and the extent to which your delivery aligned to the lesson plan

- The outcomes generated by your assessment strategies and materials and the extent to which they aligned to your planned or expected outcomes.

Awarding organisation requirements

Assessment criterion 5.1: "Review the effectiveness of own delivery of inclusive teaching and learning."

This should cover the following:

- The choice and application of teaching, learning, assessment and differentiation strategies
- The quantity and quality of verbal and non-verbal communication with learners
- Level of learner engagement and participation in the session
- Appropriate timing and pace of the micro-teach delivery
- Meeting of session objectives.

Assessment criterion 5.2: "Identify areas for improvement in own delivery of inclusive teaching and learning"

When considering areas for improvement, you should focus on the following:

- Quality and currency of subject knowledge
- Alternative approaches to planning, teaching, learning, assessment and differentiation
- Timing and pace of delivery
- Managing individual and/or group activities
- Learner-centred approaches
- Verbal and non-verbal communication skills

---

[1] The laptop could be plugged into a large screen LED television using an HDMI cable from the laptop to the television in place of a data projector. In a panel interview, this could well be the temporary set-up, especially if delivery is in a non-teaching room.

Adopting a robust and employment focused approach to evaluation

If your intention extends beyond meeting the minimum requirements of the course for the micro-teach evaluation, then the following categories can be considered:

Research and consultation

- Was the selection of the topic effective (i.e. were the prospective audience consulted)?
- To what extent did the prior learning, knowledge and experience of the audience influence the:
  - teaching, learning, assessment and differentiation strategies
  - the topic area selected
  - timing of delivery
  - the resources selected
  - the support strategies considered?
- To what extent were professional standards, codes of practice and inspection frameworks considered at the research stage?
- How effective was your research of the learning provider before the interview?

Planning

- Does the lesson plan include appropriate strategies for managing health and safety, equality and diversity and reasonable adjustments
- Were clear session and assessment objectives set and implemented?
- Were effective teaching, learning, assessment and differentiation strategies selected?
- Were the timings adhered to during delivery; if not, why not?
- Were the resources effectively deployed, according to the lesson plan?

Delivery and assessment

- Were all learners engaged and sufficiently challenged by the subject matter and assessments during the session?
- Was positive body language used throughout?

- Were group work and assessment activities effectively managed?
- Was feedback during checking of learning and assessment constructive and detailed (including use of summative and formative feedback, as appropriate)?
- Did the pace of delivery have the desired impact?
- Were session objectives clearly outlined and checked during or by the end of the session?
- Did the session have an effective structure?
- Were the room layout, learning environment and learning materials conducive to learning?
- Were reasonable adjustments fully implemented and what was their impact on those affected?

Improvement and development

A robust approach to this area could include considering the evaluation above and then identifying strengths and areas of good practice and how these can be maintained. Areas for improvement can also be identified, with clear strategies and appropriate time frames for them to be implemented. You could also consider how the effectiveness of the improvements and continuing professional development could be monitored, evaluated and reviewed.

This approach would provide an underpinning framework for assessing the impact of improvement strategies.

In relation to job interviews, there is a reasonable probability that you will attend a number of interviews before securing the lecturing or training position that you desire. It is therefore important that you maximise your learning from each interview and reflect critically before your next interview.

I recall attending a 'warm-up' interview for a lecturing position at a learning provider. I say 'warm-up' because the position I desired was at a different learning provider and the interview was scheduled four weeks after the 'warm-up' interview. It was a blisteringly hot day, with no air conditioning and seven other candidates, including three internal candidates, seated in the same room. The interview comprised of a 10 minutes micro-teach session to the interview panel, which included a teaching and learning coordinator, a middle manager and the principal. There was an interview immediately following the micro-teach. I was offered the position that afternoon, with pay at the top of the lecturer scale, which was slightly more then the other position I had in mind and for considerably less work.

The guidance to take away from this anecdote is to attend as many interviews as possible, learn from them and if offered a position consider it seriously. There was no guarantee that I would have been offered the other position. As it later transpired, this position was ideal for my subsequent career progression.

Recording the evaluation and improvement and development (course and job interview related)

Your programme tutor is likely to provide you with the necessary proforma to record the evaluation and improvements and development related plan.

If you are considering something that has more of an employment focus, then the earlier points can be arranged on a spreadsheet and updated after each interview. It would be advisable to make a note of the questions you were asked during interview shortly after the interview, regardless of the outcome. This is because themes in some questions can be repeated in subsequent interviews, especially if they are based on changes to inspection or government policy. You will then end-up with a pool of questions and possible responses in readiness for the next interview.

———————————

Nabeel's other publications:

Education and Training series:

Achieving your Award in Education and Training: The Comprehensive Course Companion (Special Edition)

Achieving your Award in Education and Training: The Comprehensive Course Companion

Meeting the Assessment Requirements of the Award in Education and Training

Award in Education and Training series:

Understanding Roles, Responsibilities and Relationships in Education and Training (Book 1)

Understanding and Using Inclusive Teaching and Learning Approaches in Education and Training (Book 2)

Understanding Assessment in Education and Training (Book 3)

Unit PASS guide for the Award in Education and Training series:

Understanding Roles, Responsibilities and Relationships in Education and Training

Understanding and Using Inclusive Teaching and Learning Approaches in Education and Training

Understanding Assessment in Education and Training

Certificate in Education and Training series:

Understanding Roles, Responsibilities and Relationships in Education and Training (Book 1)

Unit PASS guide for the Certificate in Education and Training series:

Understanding Roles, Responsibilities and Relationships in Education and Training

Equality and Diversity series:

Embedding Equality and Diversity into a Postgraduate Management Programme for International Students - a case study

Glossary of terms

Term	Definition
Accreditation of prior learning (APL)	APL is the generic term for the accreditation of prior learning, whether the result of a formal course or learning through experience. (APL is the term normally used by awarding bodies, such as universities. The equivalent used by awarding organisations is RPL.)
Accreditation of prior certificated learning (APCL)	APCL is based on certified (or certificated) learning following a formal course of study at another learning provider or institute. (APCL is the term normally used by awarding bodies, such as universities.)
Accreditation of prior experiential learning (APEL)	APEL is based on experiential learning - learning achieved through experience, rather than on a formal course of study. (APEL is the term normally used by awarding bodies, such as universities.)
Assessment criteria	Each learning outcome contains assessment criteria that are used to assess the learner evidence submitted. These are normally related to grades.
Assessor	This refers to the person responsible for making decisions about whether learners' work achieves the national standard required for certification (e.g. whether assessment criteria and any related grade descriptors have been met).
Awarding body	Although the terms awarding body and awarding organisation have been used to mean the same thing, an awarding body is normally an organisation with degree awarding powers, such as a university.
Awarding organisation	Although the terms awarding organisation and awarding body have been used to mean the same thing, awarding organisations are normally regulated by Ofqual and do not possess degree awarding powers.
Command verb	This is a verb that requires a specific action and is normally placed at the beginning of an assessment criteria, such as 'outline', 'describe', 'explain', 'analyse', 'evaluate'.

Term	Definition
Differentiation	This can be viewed as the process by which differences between learners are accommodated so that all students in a group have the best possible chance of learning. It can be divided into 7 categories, including differentiation by **task** (different tasks or exercises for different ability ranges), by **grouping** (mixed-ability groups), by **resources** (varying resources according to learner needs and abilities, such as providing basic resources and complex/advanced resources), by **pace** (learners working at a different pace can be given support or more challenging activities, so that whether a learner is falling behind, keeping up or completing exercises early in a session, support and extension materials ensure that all learners maintain momentum), by **outcome** (all students undertake the same task, but a range of results / grades are expected and considered as acceptable), by **dialogue and support** (identifying which learners need detailed explanations in simple language and which learners can engage in dialogue at a more sophisticated level. The teacher may also use directed questioning to produce a range of responses and use difficult follow-up questions to challenge the more able learners), and by **assessment** (learners are assessed on an on-going basis so that teaching, and the other methods of differentiation, can be continuously adjusted according to the learners' needs).
Diversity	There is no fixed or legal definition for diversity. It can be viewed as recognising and celebrating difference.
Equality	"Equality is about ensuring that every individual has an equal opportunity to make the most of their lives and talents, and believing that no one should have poorer life chances because of where, what or whom they were born, what they believe, or whether they have a disability." http://www.equalityhumanrights.com/private-and-public-sector-guidance/education-providers/secondary-education-resources/useful-information/understanding-equality
Learning aims/outcomes	This is what the learner should know, understand or be able to do as a result of completing the unit.
Lesson plans	A lesson plan is a lecturer's guide to delivering a particular session, including session aims, objectives, assessment strategies, session content and timeframe, learning resources to be used and lecturer and learner activities.

Term	Definition
Ofqual	The Office of Qualifications and Examinations Regulation (Ofqual) regulates qualifications, examinations and assessments in England and vocational qualifications in Northern Ireland. Ofqual is a non-ministerial department.
Pedagogy / pedagogical	These are the methods and practices in teaching, especially of children (up to the age of 18), where the focus is on the teacher's methods of transferring knowledge to a learner, who is dependent on the teacher's methods and understanding. The teacher controls the learning experience for children, and most teaching is based on a rigid curricula. A great deal of importance is placed on the grades achieved.
Peer assessment	Peer assessment involves learners taking responsibility for assessing the work of their peers against set assessment criteria.
Programme specification	"A programme specification is a concise description of the intended learning outcomes of a [higher education] programme, and the means by which the outcomes are achieved and demonstrated. In general, modules or other units of study have stated outcomes, often set out in handbooks provided by the institutions to inform student choice. These intended learning outcomes relate directly to the curriculum, study and assessment methods and criteria used to assess performance.", QAA (2006): *Guidelines for preparing programme specifications*, The Quality Assurance Agency for Higher Education, http://www.qaa.ac.uk/en/Publications/Documents/Guidelines-for-preparing-programme-specifications.pdf
Qualification specification	awarding organisations publish qualification specifications for their centres / learning providers to use in developing and delivering the awarding organisation courses. The qualification specification sets out what is required of the learner in order to achieve the qualification, it contains information about permitted unit combinations and information specific to managing and delivering the qualification(s) including specific quality assurance requirements.
Reasonable adjustment	In the context of learning providers, a reasonable adjustment is an alteration that a learning provider makes to enable a disabled learner to continue to carry out their duties without being at a disadvantage compared to other learners.

Term	Definition
Recognition of prior learning (RPL)	RPL recognises prior learning, whether the result of a formal course of study or learning through experience. RPL is the term used by awarding organisations and is equivalent to APL.
Schemes of work	A scheme of work is a guideline that defines the structure and content of a course. It maps out clearly how resources (e.g. books, equipment, time) and class activities (e.g. lecturing, group work, practicals, discussions) and assessment strategies (e.g. tests, assignments, homework) will be used to ensure that the learning outcomes and assessment criteria or assessment objectives of the course are met successfully. It will normally include times and dates. The scheme of work is usually an interpretation of a qualification specification and unit or module guides.
Self-assessment	Self-assessment requires learners to reflect on their own work and judge how well they have performed in relation to the assessment criteria.
Unit guide	These outline the unit aims, learning outcomes, assessment criteria, unit content, grading criteria and provide some guidance.
Value added measures / data	These are used to estimate or quantify how much of a positive or negative impact individual lecturers have had on student learning during the course of the programme or a year.

Appendix 1: Award in Education and Training unit learning outcomes and assessment criteria

Unit title: **Understanding Roles, Responsibilities and Relationships in Education and Training**			
Learning outcomes		**Assessment criteria**	
1.	Understand the teaching role and responsibilities in education and training	1.1	Explain the teaching role and responsibilities in education and training
		1.2	Summarise key aspects of legislation, regulatory requirements and codes of practice relating to own role and responsibilities
		1.3	Explain ways to promote equality and value diversity
		1.4	Explain why it is important to identify and meet individual learner needs
2.	Understand ways to maintain a safe and supportive learning environment	2.1	Explain ways to maintain a safe and supportive learning environment
		2.2	Explain why it is important to promote appropriate behaviour and respect for others
3.	Understand the relationships between teachers and other professionals in education and training	3.1	Explain how the teaching role involves working with other professionals
		3.2	Explain the boundaries between the teaching role and other professional roles
		3.3	Describe points of referral to meet the individual needs of learners

Appendix 1 (cont.)

Unit title: **Understanding and Using Inclusive Teaching and Learning Approaches in Education and Training**		
Learning outcomes	**Assessment criteria**	
1. Understand inclusive teaching and learning approaches in education and training	1.1	Describe features of inclusive teaching and learning
	1.2	Compare the strengths and limitations of teaching and learning approaches used in own area of specialism in relation to meeting individual learner
	1.3	Explain why it is important to provide opportunities for learners to develop their English, mathematics, ICT and wider skills
2. Understand ways to create an inclusive teaching and learning environment	2.1	Explain why it is important to create an inclusive teaching and learning environment
	2.2	Explain why it is important to select teaching and learning approaches, resources and assessment methods to meet individual learner needs
	2.3	Explain ways to engage and motivate learners
	2.4	Summarise ways to establish ground rules with learners
3. Be able to plan inclusive teaching and learning	3.1	Devise an inclusive teaching and learning plan
	3.2	Justify own selection of teaching and learning approaches, resources and assessment methods in relation to meeting individual learner needs
4. Be able to deliver inclusive teaching and learning	4.1	Use teaching and learning approaches, resources and assessment methods to meet individual learner needs
	4.2	Communicate with learners in ways that meet their individual needs
	4.3	Provide constructive feedback to learners to meet their individual needs
5. Be able to evaluate the delivery of inclusive teaching and learning	5.1	Review the effectiveness of own delivery of inclusive teaching and learning
	5.2	Identify areas for improvement in own delivery of inclusive teaching and learning

Unit title: **Understanding Assessment in Education and Training**		
Learning outcomes	**Assessment criteria**	
1. Understand types and methods of assessment used in education and training	1.1	Explain the purposes of types of assessment used in education and training
	1.2	Describe characteristics of different methods of assessment in education and training
	1.3	Compare the strengths and limitations of different assessment methods in relation to meeting individual learner needs
	1.4	Explain how different assessment methods can be adapted to meet individual learner needs
2. Understand how to involve learners and others in the assessment process	2.1	Explain why it is important to involve learners and others in the assessment process
	2.2	Explain the role and use of peer- and self-assessment in the assessment process
	2.3	Identify sources of information that should be made available to learners and others involved in the assessment process
3. Understand the role and use of constructive feedback in the assessment process	3.1	Describe key features of constructive feedback
	3.2	Explain how constructive feedback contributes to the assessment process
	3.3	Explain ways to give constructive feedback to learners
4. Understand requirements for keeping records of assessment in education and training	4.1	Explain the need to keep records of assessment of learning
	4.2	Summarise the requirements for keeping records of assessment in an organisation

Printed in Great Britain
by Amazon